# Bits, Bitting and Spanish Horses

Bits, Bitting and Spanish Horses

THE CHIEF ROJAS FACT BOOK
ABOUT SUCCESSFUL HORSE
TRAINING AND THE PROPER USE
OF EQUIPMENT

by

A. R. Rojas

KIMBERLY PRESS, INC.
Goleta, California

This book is a complete, unabridged edition of the original classic by Arnold R. Rojas. We have kept it exactly as the edition he published in 1970. Rojas was 74.
He passed away eighteen years later in 1988.

The publisher wishes to thank Mr. Rojas' family, especially Ms. Juanita Montes for help in this project.
We thank you, the reader, for your interest in the work of this important author.

William C. Reynolds, Publisher
Alamar Media, Inc.
Santa Ynez, California
www.oldcowdogs.com

Copyright © 2010 - Alamar Media, Inc.
Printed in the United States of America
All Rights Reserved

ISBN: 978-0-615-42697-6

*Dedicated to John Bacon and his sister
Heloise Bacon Powers, Californians*

ACKNOWLEDGEMENT

I must not forget to thank Jim Day, Ralph Krieser, and Walter Kane for their generous help and encouragement.

Arnold Rojas

CONTENTS

1	BITS AND BITTING	19
2	THE SPANISH HORSE	31
3	INDIAN HORSES	48
4	OLD TIMERS AND SUCH	53
5	THE BROWN VAQUERO HORSE	64
6	HORSES AND HORSEMEN	71
7	THERE ARE TRICKS IN ALL TRADES	76
8	STORIES AND SKETCHES	80
	A Strike for Higher Wages	80
	Appaloosa	84
	Spanish Cattle	86
	Wisdom	88
	Fiesta	89
	Portrait of a Pioneer	91
	Ranch Horses	92
	Seris	93
	Cantleberry	95
	The Lazy Mule	97
	Pete Rivera	99

Illustrations: Spurs and bits on pages 62 and 63. A gallery of rare illustrations begins following page 64.

INTRODUCTION

In the preparation of this work the author has had certain advantages. He can speak the language of the vaquero (Spanish) and the language of the Anglo buckaroo (English). He has had access to the records of cattle companies which existed during the period under consideration. He has had the opportunity to consult old men who lived through the West's formative years. He has derived aid from writers on subjects connected with the life of the vaquero and buckaroo. He has enjoyed acquaintance among those who are directly descended from the original colonists, and especially among the descendants of those who lived at the time treated. He is, in fact, related by blood to many of them. He has travelled in Latin America, Spain, Portugal and Morocco and has consulted the foremost breeders and authorities in those countries with respect to their horses.

He has been enabled, in many cases, to verify the incidents which were related to him, and in other instances has been able to compare traditional reports with written records; and from these sources has compiled the scenes, incidents and adventures of the persons of whom he writes.

He has studied the records and catalogs of the numerous saddleries which were in business for over a century. These throw light upon the genesis of the cattle industry and questions of interest connected with the vaquero and buckaroo.

With all due sense of his faults, he cherishes the hope that he has succeeded in evoking an image of the range rider of that period which is consistent with the truth.

The range rider of the West—vaquero and buckaroo—has been a part of the American scene for almost two centuries; yet it is a curious fact that misconceptions regarding him are more glaring than those of other more remote historical figures.

This work may be called the story of the men of the West;

and though it deals in large part with California it may properly be accepted as the story of most range riders west of the Rocky Mountains. Men who could wear a pair of denim pants and a chambray shirt with a distinction which no man, least of all a workman, has ever worn clothing; whose method of working was unique among herdsmen; men who, in a sense, lived a life of make-believe wherein they were bound by what they thought a vaquero should be, and with this thought in mind, took their slick-fork saddles, rawhide reatas and peculiar methods of working over half a continent.

Those who read these pages may ask why the author always speaks tenderly of the men, horses and places of whom and of which he writes. He can answer that by simply stating that every one of the vaqueros and buckaroos with whom he worked was a better man than he was. Contrary to the "western" formula, he did not, on his arrival among them, ride their worst outlaw horse to a quivering surrender; nor rescue a beautiful girl from the clutches of a villain. As a matter of fact, he never could have ridden their worst outlaw at any time during his years among them. The foremen, bless their hearts, in the wisdom born of years of handling would-be vaqueros, knew his abilities—or rather his shortcomings—better than he knew them himself. They gave him horses that would remain docilely horizontal on the coldest mornings and would keep their footing whether jogging along the steepest mountainsides or racing after a beef over terrain pitted with squirrel holes; horses that would carry him faithfully to the end of the longest rodeo day, take up their responsibility when a cow was parted out of the herd, their rider sitting in complete bewilderment on the saddle, and guide the cow to the *parada*. In a word, a horse that could, and would, teach his rider.

Now as to beautiful girls waiting to be rescued from villains and other perils, to state a truth, they were very, very scarce. Any girls to be found on ranches had more sense than to place themselves in a villain's path and those who did, either by accident or by design, would probably have resented interference. Besides, in those days, the villain himself would have been the first to shoot any man who molested a woman.

It may be said, by way of criticism, that this work is overburdened with the history of Spain and Spanish horses; but only by including it in the text can the reader see the panorama of California's pastoral heritage unfold before his eyes. The author is also aware that this subject has been treated many times; but he believes this to be a rare work in that it brings the vaquero and his gringo comrade the buckaroo, his history, his customs, his tools and methods of handling cattle and horses, and above all, his origins, between two covers.

The author's sincere gratitude goes to the many people who have made this work possible. High on a long list which must remain incomplete are the following: Bernice Harrell Chipman and Walter Kane, of the *Bakersfield Californian*, for permission to use the stories published in that newspaper; Francisco Montaño D.V.M. of Sevilla, Spain, technical director of the sales, breeding and exportation of Andalusian horses, for much of the history on Spanish horses; Don Manuel Guerrero Y Gonzales of Jerez, Spain, and Fernando Terry Merello (the Irish Spaniard) of Puerto Santa Maria, Spain, breeders of Andalusian horses; Joa De Menezes Mourao of Lisbon, Portugal for help in studying the Portuguese horses; Kharchafi Mohamed of Fez, Morocco, for help in studying the horses of Barbary; Bob Robertson of Carson City, Nevada, Henry Schipman Jr. of Las Cruces, New Mexico, Chuck Hitchcock of Shafter, California, and Louis Hengehold of Santa Paula, California who valiantly stood up for him when the deluge of criticism fell thick and heavy on this author's old head; Kay Young of San Diego who prepared the manuscript, and last but not least the vaqueros and buckaroos such as Tom Ramoss who have had so large a part in this work and who told him the stories so that the California tradition may not die away.

A. R. Rojas
Santa Barbara
MAY 1, 1970

Bits, Bitting and Spanish Horses

CHAPTER 1

BITS AND BITTING

Through the centuries the handling and using of horses has been the hardest and cruelest of all human practices. Victims of indifference and cruelty through the ages, horses have been beaten to death, starved to death, worked to death.

Some of this abuse could not have been avoided of course; but much of it was caused by man's indifference and inhumanity.

Horses have been driven into lines of spears, lances, pikes, bayonets, belching cannon, and rifle fire. They have been slaughtered on the world's battlefields since time immemorial.

Through the centuries horses have been jerked out of the way of blows aimed at their riders, and have suffered untold abuse to their mouths so that their riders might stay alive.

More lives, of both men and horses have been lost on the battlefields as the result of the bad management of horses than by all the sword strokes, lance thrusts, or flights of arrows.

Bitting is one of man's oldest problems, and the eternal search for a bit that will give complete control of the horse has been going on through the centuries, and oddly enough more horses have been spoiled by bad bitting than by any other cause.

The handling and training of horses has been, through the ages, one of the most important of professions because so many lives depended on the management of horses. Indeed, it was so important that certain orders of the priesthood became the trainers of warhorses.

We know that the lever is one of the oldest mechanical principles discovered by man; but we do not know at what period in history ancient horsemen got the idea of using leverage to stop a horse.

The discovery may have occurred when the horses those ancient horsemen were riding stampeded into the ranks of the enemy, or when the management of horses became important in warfare. The science of bitting horses is one of the oldest cultures known to Semitic peoples, and has been studied by military men since the dawn of history. The Moors took it to Spain in the eighth century. The Crusaders met the Saracens riding horses with curb bits in Palestine in the eleventh century. Books on the art of bitting horses, written in Spanish and in Arabic, have been published in Spain since the ninth century, and in the New World since the sixteenth.

The curb bit, as we know it, probably made its way from Egypt to Phoenicia and from there to the Phoenician colonies in North Africa; and we know that it is old because horses on Assyrian and Greek sculptures are depicted with mouths that have been pried open with curb bits. The freize of the Parthenon is an example. The trigger-reined horse which was brought to America by Spaniards was trained for use in war and not for use as a cowhorse. The reined cowhorse evolved from the cavalryman's horse in later years. Those old-time horsemen were unique among herdsmen in developing the bit as a signaling device and not as a lever.

Diego De Ybarra, the conquistadore, brought the finest horses that could be found in Spain first to Durango and then to Sonora. From there the horses came to California where the skill of the reinsman and the quality of the "Spanish Horse" reached the highest degree of refinement in New Spain. For a hundred years travelers to the West Coast have written in praise of California horses and of a horsemanship, faint traces of which exist to this day.

A bit, the measurements of which may suit one horse perfectly, may not suit another. For that reason bits with different leverages are perpetually being made, and the manufacturing of bits is a great industry. A bit with shanks in the form of an S may take a pull of four pounds to put thirty-two pounds of pressure against the chinstrap, while a bit with less leverage, one with straight shanks such as a Las Cruces or a Santa Barbara, will require a pull of twenty-four pounds to put thirty-two pounds of pressure against the chinstrap.

The severity of a bit is all in the length of the shank. But a horse's mouth will suffer just as much from a bit that has insufficient leverage and has to be pulled or jerked hard as he will from a bit that has the proper leverage and that requires a slight pull.

If a five pound bit is put in a ten pound mouth, the horse will disregard it to the extent of bearing on it. On the other hand if a ten pound bit is put in a five pound mouth the horse will suffer from too much bit. It is when the horse is bitted properly and the rider and horse have developed an affinity to each other that the bit becomes a signaling device and ceases being a lever.

In order that a horse should become well-reined he must be prepared for the bit if he is to work on it, and if a horse does not work on a bit it is because he has not been prepared for it. Horses have soft or hard, tough or tender mouths. Men have soft or hard, tough or tender hands, and the result is the good or bad behavior of the horse.

The art of handling a horse effectively is complicated and difficult, and is largely a matter of natural instinct and certainly cannot be learned out of a book. Even the best horsemen have to make a great effort to master it. Undoubtedly there are aptitudes for horsemanship, but nowhere is work and patience more effective than in training horses, and if patience is the key to heaven it is also the key to a well trained horse.

There is no ideal way of training a horse. The training depends on the disposition of the animal and on that of the rider. No set method is worth anything; for no two horses or riders are alike and methods found in books are utter nonsense. Charlatans have done endless harm with their books of instructions on how to train horses. Such books encourage people who have no natural fitness for it to undertake the training of horses. Training is an intricate science for which many people have no talent. Horses differ radically in disposition and intelligence just as men differ. Every horse cannot be a prize winner, and by the same token, every rider cannot be a Jimmy Williams, an M. R. Valdez, or a C. W. Neil.

A horse can be trained in any way that is fitting. In Europe a horse is trained with a *cavesson*, in Argentina with a *Tira De Bocado* (a strap or cord tied around the lower jaw), in England with a snaffle bit, in the American West (California, Oregon, and Nevada) with a *jaquima* (a rawhide noseband). Each method leads to the same result. Polo is the supreme test of a good horse; yet good polo horses are found in England, in Argentina, in California. True, there are time-honored methods which horsemen have used through the centuries to subdue horses; but even the most time-proven will have different effects, and besides, those methods were used by experienced men who knew when they had reached the limit of their effectiveness.

A horse will not suddenly lose all his bad habits and become well trained by the simple process of putting a snaffle bit in his mouth and riding him with it, as one man who writes on the training of the "Western" horse claims. More horses have been spoiled and more tongues have been cut with a snaffle bit than by any other device used to train horses: because if a colt bucks or runs away he will of necessity have to be pulled, and the result will be a cut or bruised mouth.

The action of any curb bit, whether of high or low port is never on the roof of the horse's mouth. The action is on the tongue and bars. However high the port of a bit may be, the action of the chinstrap or chain allows the port to go only so far in the horse's mouth. Since there's about two inches of space between the bottom and the roof of the animal's mouth, the port cannot hit the roof unless the chinstrap should happen to break—a remote possibility—or is left off the bit altogether, which should never be done.

The mouthpiece which has a straight bar instead of "tongue space" is the least severe because the horse uses its tongue to cushion or absorb the shock; he balls his tongue against the bit when it is pulled against the bars.

All mouthpieces, whatever their shape, have but one function, and that is to bear on the tongue and bars of the mouth to inflict pain. The only time the bit does not inflict pain in its function as a lever is when the horse has a mouth so sensitive that the bit can be used as a signaling device and is pulled only hard enough to give a signal. This was the original purpose of the spade bit. But when the mouth once becomes numbed by hard and constant pulling the shape of the mouthpiece will mean very little when the bit is pulled, because the degree of severity depends on the pull and on the length of the shanks.

By the same token, the act of putting a certain form of mouthpiece in a horse's mouth does not presuppose that the animal will become well-reined, quit throwing his head, and turn and stop perfectly.

However, there are three mouthpieces that can inflict very severe pain; they are English bits, adopted, no doubt, at one time or another, from the Hispanic-Mauresque culture. One is the universal snaffle bit, another is the S shaped U. S. Army cavalry bit, the third is the bit used by the Buckingham Palace guards. It has a hight port shaped like as inverted V which bears down on the bars of a horse's mouth in a squeezing action.

The knowledge of bitting is of utmost importance, yet it is the least understood. The bit is a precision tool which should be the most understood of the rider's equipment. There are numerous styles and designs of bits. Many are useful, but just as many are worthless. Some are foisted on horsemen as miracle bits which can eliminate all the bad habits a horse has acquired through bad handling. They are bought, tried, then discarded for some other miracle bit which is as worthless as the first.

Most riders buy bits in the fond hope that they will work, without the rider taking the trouble to learn their function. There are tons of discarded bits and hundreds of spoiled horses that could have been made useful if the riders would have given a little thought to the matter of bits and made an effort to study their action in a horse's mouth. Good horsemen are not made by miracle bits. True, better bits enable a horseman to do a better job; but an unskilled horseman cannot do a good job, no matter what bit he uses, because there are no miracle bits.

Some bits have high ports, and some hardly give any ports at all but only a curve in the center of the mouthpiece—"tongue space" as it is called. The degree of obedience the horse will give is decided by the degree of sensibility to pressure applied to the mouth. This pressure has little effect on the chin groove, because it is less sensitive than the tongue and bars.

The horse's lower jaw consists of two triangular jawbones covered with a layer of flesh between which the tongue lies. Horses vary in sensitivity and shape of the bars of their mouth. Some have little feeling, others are very sensitive; it follows that all horses will react differently to the pressure of a bit. A horse with a thick tongue will, of course, be less sensitive and will suffer less from a pull on the bit than a horse with a thin tongue. A bit that is too narrow will pinch the lips. A bit that is too wide will slide from one side of the mouth to the other and cause the horse to turn his head sidewise when the reins are pulled.

Since the curb bit, whatever its form, is a lever, it depends on the arrangement and the adjustment of the curb strap or chain for the action to be either good or bad. The shanks are the lever, the curb strap or chain is the fulcrum or prop lifting against the tongue and bars. Theoretically, this should pull the horse's chin in the direction of the rider's hand. However, if the leverage is wrong, if the lever (cheeks and shanks) do not correspond to the dimensions of the bars of the horse's mouth, the set of the horse's head, and the length of the horse's neck, the action will be opposite to that which is desired. The horse's head will go up instead of in the direction of the rider's hand. If the cheeks of the bit are too high, and the shanks are too short, the pull will be on the headstall and poll and not on the horse's mouth. The direction in which the bit acts depends on the leverage applied by the mouthpiece, the curb strap or chain, and the shanks and cheeks. If the curb strap is too loose, it will pinch the lips. If the chin or curb strap or chain is too tight, there is no leverage.

The bit is most effective when it is placed low rather than high in the horse's mouth because the action of the headstall must also be considered in the functioning of the bit. The headstall pulls the bit up and against the pull of the curb strap or chain. The mouthpiece should be placed between the grinders and croppers (molars and the incisors) and in line with the chin groove. Since horses' mouths are not all alike, each horse requires a bit adapted to his peculiar dimensions, and his reactions are decided by the amount of pressure inflicted by the bit. A bit gives a slight signal or intense pain. If the effect of the bit is in proportion to the sensitiveness of the mouth there will be no severe pain, only a signal which the horse should take.

A bit with a curb strap or chain that is too tight will cause a horse to fret and throw his head. Many of the problems of bitting are caused by the bad adjustment of the curb strap or chain. There should be enough room to allow the second finger of the right hand to pass between the curb strap or chain and the chin; otherwise there will be no leverage. Moreover, there must be an arch of thirty-five degrees in the shanks of the bit before leverage can be applied.

A horse has a good mouth when it reacts to the most delicate pressure on the bit. A horse has a bad mouth when it responds only to a hard pull or a jerk on the reins. A horse has a spoiled mouth when it does not react to a pull on the reins or when the mouth is excessively tender or so excessively hard that it is insensible to the pressure of a bit.

If a spade or a grazer bit is put in a horse's mouth, one or the other will perform the function for which the bit is made as long as the horse is sensitive to a pull on the bit. Therefore, it is not which bit is used, but how it is used. The severest form of bit is that which has "tongue space." When a pull is exerted on a bit with such a mouthpiece, the blow falls on the bars of the mouth and is not absorbed by the tongue which is the fleshiest part of the mouth and the least sensitive. Another instrument of useless torture is the bit with the low, wide port. This contrivance has a pinching action on the bars, and the pull on one rein will press on one or the other of the bars and cause useless pain. This mouthpiece, because of its design, is always getting lopsided in the horse's mouth. All old-time riders knew this and would use bits with straight bar mouthpieces only, that is to say, bits that did not have tongue space. The proof is that most of the old style bits found today have straight bar mouthpieces.

A bit with a horizontal slit to hold the headstall was never favored by old time riders, because the pull on the reins and bit was conveyed to the headstall and poll and interfered with the action of the bit. They preferred a bit with a ring rather than one with a slit.

To sum up: the pull on the rein is the effect of the mouthpiece, the cheeks and shanks, the curb strap or chain, the headstall and above all, the muscular strength of the rider. It is an interesting and pertinent fact that old time riders, who used a bit with a straight bar mouthpiece never had to change bits, even after they had used the same bit on the same horse for the animal's lifetime.

The snaffle bit is the oldest bit known to Europeans. Spaniards were using snaffle bits for a thousand years before they came to the Americas, but the fact remains that they developed the *cavesson* and the *jaquima* to keep from tearing up the mouths of horses that had become wild in the New World. When a snaffle bit is used for any length of time on a horse, the animal will acquire the habit of raising its nose and bringing the bit against its molars to relieve pressure on the tongue and bars. "Western" horses that have been started with a snaffle bit instead of a *jaquima* never fail to be "high headed," that is, throw their heads up instead of downward when they feel the pull on the reins, a habit difficult to correct. The pull on the snaffle which is crosswise of the tongue and bars, wrecks more mouths than any curb bit that was ever devised. And the snaffle mouthpiece when made into a leverage bit is one of the severest because it has a pincer movement on the bars. The jointed mouthpiece takes the form of an inverted V. The snaffle, if it does not have a chin strap to hold it, will slide across the tongue and bars and through the mouth.

The size, weight, length of the horse's head and the angle at which it is set are factors in deciding the animal's action, as much as other parts of the animal's anatomy. The horse's head acts on the neck and the rest of the body, and if the head is stretched out or bowed down into the animal's chest there will be little control and the bit will be ineffective. In other words, if the head is too high or too low control over the horse is lost.

Another problem is for the horse to become adjusted to the weight of his rider. An immature horse cannot be expected to adjust himself to the added weight and to a bit at the same time. The old time ranch rider is often ridiculed as a horseman, but the fact remains that he knew enough to ride a colt in the jaquima until the animal had adjusted himself to the added weight on his back.

There is nothing in the action of putting a certain type of bit in a horse's mouth which presupposes that the end result will be a perfectly reined horse. The prying of a piece of steel against the tender parts of a horse's mouth often results in confusion because of lack of proper bitting and the rider's lack of experience in handling the reins. Neither is it true that by putting a certain type of mouthpiece in a horse's mouth the animal will suddenly become well reined, stop throwing its head, and stop opening its mouth when a pull on the bit is exerted.

True, a certain type of mouthpiece may press less on a sore or lacerated part of a horse's mouth, just as a dental plate will press less when it has been cut down to relieve pressure on a nerve but the end effect of the curb bit is decided by the length of its shank and cheek, and not by the shape of the mouthpiece.

While one curb bit has the same action as another, the difference in leverage go from one extreme to another. One bit may have but little leverage while another may have enough to "lift a boxcar."

I do not make bold to set down rules, or to make a rule. This is just what I have observed in a lifetime spent among horses and horsemen. In a period of over fifty years I have seen the best and worst of horse masters. I have ridden with men who rode horses with spade and riding bits and needle sharp spurs; yet their pride in an ages-old tradition of horsemanship prevented them from over cutting a tongue or slashing a flank. And, by the same token, I have ridden with men who mauled a horse's mouth into a bloody, lifeless pulp with a snaffle bit.

The men who understood the function of the curb bit tried to use its bruising power as little as possible. They avoided pulling on the bit, by guiding their horse with their legs. They saw an analogy in the horse's mouth and a workman's hands. The old-time riders learned very early in their experiences with horses that the more a rider pulled on a horse's mouth, the harder and less sensitive the horse's mouth would become, just as a man's hands will become hard and calloused from the continual contact with the handle of a shovel or a hoe.

The Indians and vaqueros on Tejon Ranch—when Don Jesus Lopez was majordomo—were masters of horse psychology. Every colt they rode was subjected to an intense study; and the names those Indians gave them were an indication of how well the Indians had learned their horse's characteristics or disposition. They used signals and leg pressure to guide a horse even after the horse was in the bridle. They knew that as long as the colt did not become hard on the hackamore, he would not have to be pulled on the bit. It was only after a colt began to lug or pull on the hackamore that the bit was used. But by that time the horse was thoroughly trained.

Years ago, when I first went to work on Tejon Ranch there were some horse-wise Indians among the vaqueros. One was Nacho Montes, who during his lifetime had already become a legend as a *jinete* (rider of bucking horses). The other was Nepmuseno (Cheno) Cordero. Of the two I liked Cheno because he condescended to ride with me when the other Indians remained aloof. (Indians are the hardest people in the world to become acquainted with. In after years I was to act often as the chief of the Tejon Indians; but that is another story). Cheno was the exact opposite of Nacho. While Nacho was, or had been a *jinete,* Cheno could not ride a bucking horse. If a horse gave the mildest crowhop, Cheno would be thrown; yet Don Jesus would pick the finest, most promising colts on the ranch and give them to Cheno to ride; for he had an infinite patience with a horse. Twenty years after I had left the Tejon Ranch, I had the privilege of riding an old Tejon horse which the Indian had started. Although the horse had been sold because he had become too feeble for the work on the ranch he still had as sweet a mouth as any horse I have ever ridden. He was at least twenty-five years old.

Cheno was short and fat and almost as broad as he was long. His legs were much too short for his body. Don Jesus said, facetiously, of course, that the Indian was so heavy and broad across the hips that if a bucking horse ever got his seat out of the saddle it would be too heavy to get back into the saddle again, and that was why Cheno got bucked off.

Cheno studied his horses and always got the best results with the least amount of friction. Since I ride out with him in the morning—colts go better in company with another horse— I was able to watch every move he made in turning out a good horse. Every morning we would ride out and away from the other vaqueros. When we had reached a secluded place, preferably a flat sandy stretch of ground, the Indian would school his horse. First, he would turn the colt crosswise of the sun. At that time of day (sunup) the sun's shadows are verticle and long, and the Indian could watch his shadow and see the position of the colt's legs. He would get the colt into a fast run, and when the colt was fully extended Cheno would reach down and get a short hold on the right rein, squeeze his legs and pull the colt to a stop. He would then turn the colt around, get him into a run again and when the colt was extended the Indian would reach down, get a short hold on the left rein this time, squeeze his legs, and pull the colt to a stop again. The colt never failed to slide to a stop because his legs were in the right position and Cheno never failed to pull when the colt's hind legs were extended under its body and its forehand was in the air, that is to say, off the ground. The Indian would pull the colt two times, once to the right and once to the left, never any more and he schooled the colt only once a day.

The morning came when the Indian could race the colt for a distance, squeeze his legs, raise the rein, but without pulling, bring the colt to a smooth, sliding stop. From that moment Cheno never pulled that colt again. Every morning afterwards, when we had ridden out and he was ready to *remanger*, as vaqueros call this phase of training, he would dismount, take a strap and tie the stirrups under the horse's body. He would then mount, get the colt crosswise of the sun and go through the stopping process again. But this time he would drop the reins and use only leg pressure to stop the horse.

At first I could not understand why he tied his stirrups; but I knew better than to ask. Indians answer such questions with, "Porque no pones cuidado? ((Why don't you observe?) Indians belive that a boy should keep his eys open and his mouth shut.

It was not until I had seen Montana and Wyoming riders tie their stirrups to ride a bucking horse and learned that tied stirrups make a fulcrum. A rider with tied stirrups can exert a much greater pressure with his legs around a horse's belly than he can without tied stirrups.

Chapter 2

THE SPANISH HORSE

Since time immemorial horses have been a cultural and economic force on the Iberian Peninsula; and a history of the Spanish horse is a history of Spain, of its heroes—Christians, Moslems, pagans—Romans, Goths, Carthaginians, Arabs, Moors, and Jews. It is a history of ruthless invasions and of fierce contests—long battles fought without quarter to the bitter end.

For many centuries Spaniards and Portuguese have bred horses that excel in the dressage of the Spanish Riding School (*La Jineta*), in the arena (*Toreo A La Jineta*), in working fighting bulls on the breeding farms, and in warfare—horses that are bred to follow blindly the will of their rider in peril on the battlefield or in the bullring, and never refuse even at the cost of their lives.

The Spanish horse is termed "Andalusian" because he was developed in the basin of Guadalquivir in the provinces of Seville, Cadiz, Huelva, Malaga, Jaen and Cordova. Students of zootechnics have concluded that two distinct groups of horses called "Andalusian" exist in Spain and Portugal. The horses of the first group are from fourteen-two to fifteen-two hands in height and weigh from 950 to 1100 pounds. They have a head which could be the result of crosses with horses brought into Spain by Germanic kings, and the native "Barb." They also have the "frightened" eyes which characterized the Norman horses which headed the royal stud at Cazorla in 1823.

The horses of the second group are the same height and weight, but they have a straight or concave profile which, contrary to widely-accepted theory, is not the result of crosses with the Arabian, Barb or any Eastern horse, but is the reward of the long and arduous labor of selective breeding.

About the only difference in the horses of the two groups is in the heads. All Andalusians have a short skull, large eyes, wide nostrils and the tapered muzzle of the medieval horse which the many outcrosses have been unable to destroy; small active ears, long necks, long oblique shoulders, deep chests, short backs with good withers, and the beautifully rounded croup with the tail set low—which is the best feature of the Andalusian horse. All have high knee action. The horses are born dark, that is to say, blue-roan, iron-gray, dark-gray, with variations of ash and roan, and turn white on reaching maturity. Bays, sorrels, browns and duns occur, but blacks are rare. Dun and bay are the preferred colors.

Andalusian horses are descended from the original grays and roans which existed in the primitive state in Spain before stone-age men settled in the peninsula. Paintings in caves and refuges of Paleolithic men show horses of convex profile of the type which, like the Iberian bull (*Bos Primigenius*), have survived and adapted themselves to modern conditions.

Although horses existed in Spain in the wild state in the time of Strabo (B.C. 63–B.C. 24?), who described them minutely, bronze-age drawings show horses domesticated and ridden with a bit. Posidonius (90 B.C.) spoke of horses in Spain as "blue-gray flecked with white, superior in speed and endurance to all other horses of the Roman Empire."

Of course, the horses that came into Spain in the various invasions crossed with the native animals, but the Spanish horse absorbed them all. Descriptions of the Iberian horse down through the ages show that the type has not been modified by outcrosses. Travellers in Spain before the time of Christ described them as having "the eye of the ox, the hoof of the ass, the mouth and throat of the wolf, the ear and tail of the fox." They said further that those horses could "turn like a serpent, walk like a cat and run like a deer."

Spaniards have always defended themselves on horseback against invaders who brought horses into Spain; and all of them—Carthaginians, Goths, Vandals, Arabs, Moors and Frenchmen—found the Spanish horses better than their own. When Hannibal, the Carthaginian general, took his Punic and Numidian horsemen into Spain he found men mounted on "sturdy" horses superior to his own. It was said of his Numidian horsemen, "Nothing was more miserable to the sight than those horsemen. The men and horses were small and feeble. The horsemen were almost naked and carried no weapons other than darts. The horses wore neither bits nor bridles, and ran with their heads and necks extended, like hounds following a scent. The horses were very swift, and toil did not tire them. They suffered from the neglect of their riders who neither cleaned them nor washed nor combed their manes or tails. Their riders never fed them, and, on ending a journey the barbarians would dismount and turn the horses out to shift for themselves."

Tarif Ben Tarif, the Moorish historian, says that when the Moors invaded Spain in the eighth century they found horses more numerous and of better quality than those in Africa, and that after winning the first battle (Guadalete) the Moors took so many horses that they changed from infantrymen to cavalrymen. He says further that after the Moors established themselves in Spain they bred Spanish horses in preference to the African horses.

For centuries the Moors and Christians carried on an intermittent war in which loot was the main objective. But when the Omeya dynasty assumed power in Moslem Spain the fighting became fiercer. At first the Christians rode *a la brida*, used heavy cavalry, armored infantry and attacked en masse. Their advantage of weight, however, was offset by the fire of the Moorish crossbowmen. The Christians were forced to fight a defensive war. The Moors, on the other hand, rode *a la jineta*, used light armor or none at all and light, fleet, enduring horses. They rode on raids out of Andalusia for long distances over the sterile Castilian Plain while the Christians stayed in their walled towns. The Moors rode mares as well as stallions and thus could select the best animals of either sex and mate them to produce war-horses.

Moslem-Christian warfare lasted for seven hundred years. Because of their need for horses that were at once swift and enduring, the Arabs and Moors had for centuries matched one horse against another in trials of speed to determine its worth in battle.

The Spaniards of southern Spain were the first to abandon their style of riding (*a la brida*) and adopt the style of the Moors; and by the time of Henry IV, "who rode *a la jineta* like any Moor," both Moor and Christian in Spain rode alike. This can be assumed because the treatises on the art of *la jineta*, written by Moors from the ninth to the fourteenth centuries were, except in the language, the same as those written by Christians during the same period.

After the manner of the Moors, the Christians matched their horses in short races to prepare them for the ceaseless, implacable warfare which went on through the centuries.

The horsemen of Jerez were among the first to change from riding *a la brida* to riding *a la jineta*. They developed a strategy which was very effective against the Moors. They would wait for the Moors to charge, then they would flee. When the Moorish lines were extended, the Jerezaños would "turn their horses on a palm of ground, as a horse is turned before a bull in the arena, and attack and slay the enemy one by one." This tactic was successfully used by Californianos against Kearney at San Pasqual several centuries later. Indeed, there has come down to us the name of a horse from those times of the Moors. His name was Chaparrillo (Shorty) and his master was Don Pedro Nuñez De Villavicencio, nicknamed El Chiquito (Little One). This Don Pedro, "small of body but great in spirit," was famous in the wars of Granada.

Eventually, the horses of Jerez had acquired such fame that Her Catholic Majesty, Queen Isabela, sent a request to the capitulars of Jerez that she be sent "the good and especial gray horse" of Juan Riguel, for to own an Andalusian was to be envied by kings. There is a letter extant from Juan II to the council of Jerez requesting that he be sent the "good sorrel horse" of Don Pedro Nuñez De Villavicenio. This request "over-flowed the measure" because the council remembered that it had recently sent the king two horses that had cost the city dear. So the council did not send the queen a horse; instead, it went on record to pay for no horses other than those used by the municipal guard.

By the time the Moors had been defeated in Granada, their last stronghold in Spain, *Genetti De Spagna* (Spanish Jennets) were the most popular warhorses in Europe and were being used to improve other breeds, as thoroughbreds are used today. After 1565 when the Andalusians were exported to Lippiza to found the Spanish Riding School, the horse became so expensive that its exportation was strictly prohibited.

Velasquez, Rubens, Titian and Gustave Dore immortalized the Andalusian on canvas and Hugo, Scott, Dumas and other writers mounted their heroes on the Andalusian horse. William the Conqueror rode an Andalusian at the battle of Hastings and Richard the Lion Hearted rode one to the Crusades. The French took great numbers of Andalusians for use in their cavalry during the Napoleonic wars. Spanish horses left their blood-stained footprints on the snow along the frozen road in the terrible retreat from Moscow, and many drowned at the crossing of the Borysthenes, carrying their masters to safety, faithful to the last. The British found them worthy and true at Balaklava, at Khartoum and in the Transvaal.

It was the Andalusian horse that made it possible for the Spaniards to gain a foothold on the American continent. And it remained for Bernal Diaz Del Castillo, a blunt old soldier of the Conquest of Mexico, to give the Andalusian horse his eulogy. In his *Historia Verdadera De La Conquista,* one of the most amazing and vivid narratives of adventure ever written, the good Bernal says, "The Conquest was made *a la jineta* and, (after God), we owed the victory to the horses."

He says of Motilla, the horse of Gonzalo De Sandoval, "He was the best horse ever to come to the New World. He was a bay with a star in his forehead, and his near foot was white. He became a legend, so that when any horse was extraordinarily good, we used to say that he was as good as Motilla. I must say of him that he was the swiftest, the best reined and the finest figure of a horse in New Spain."

There were sixteen "companions of the Conquest," eleven stallions and five mares; two of the stallions were of the finest Jineta breed of Spain.

Half a century later Bernal Diaz gives a minute description of the horses that had come in the first armada with Cortez:

"Captain Cortez: a bay stallion which died soon after we reached San Juan De Ulloa.

"Pedro De Alvarado and Hernando De Avila: a very good sorrel mare for sport and racing, and the half of which Alvarado took forcibly or brought on our arrival in New Sprin.

"Alonzo Hernando De Puertocarrera: a silver gray mare of good racing quality that Cortez bought with golden ornaments.

"Juan Velasquez De Leon: another silver gray mare, very powerful, that we called 'La Rabona' (The Rat-tailed One), very restless and a good racer.

"Cristobal De Olid: a dark chestnut stallion, very good.

"Francisco De Montejo and Alonzo De Avila: a brownish sorrel stallion, unfit for war.

"Francisco De Morla: a dark bay stallion, a great racer and very restless.

"Juan De Escalante: a light stallion with three white feet, was no good.

"Diego De Ordaz: a silver gray mare, barren, fair, but a poor racer.

"Gonzalo Dominguez: an excellent horseman, a dark bay stallion, very good and a great racer.

"Pedro Gonzalo De Trujillo: a good bay stallion, a perfect bay, that ran very well.

"Moron, a native of Vaimo: a cream-colored stallion with marked forefeet and very restless.

"Baeno, a native of Trinidad: a dun stallion with black points, does not go very well.

"Lares, a very good horseman: a very good stallion of a light bay color and a good racer.

"Ortiz the musician and Bartolome Garcia, who used to have gold mines, a very good dark bay stallion that they called 'El Arriero' (The Driver); this was one of the good horses that we carried in the fleet.

"Juan Sedeño, a native of Javana, a bay mare that foaled on the ship. At that time one could not find horses of Negroes except at their weight in gold; and the reason we did not carry more horses was that there were none."*

Time after time when the Indians had closed around, the staunch, dauntless El Romo (the Roman Nosed One), would leap into the air and kick, and thus shake off the swarms of Indians. He was the stoutest horse of the Conquest.

Alvarado brought one hundred and fifty horses when he joined Cortez at Vera Cruz and not long afterward Narvaez, the luckless one-eyed Basque, brought nine hundred and eighty, and lost them with all his men to the wily Cortez.

---

* Author's note: Because the adjective of color, *castaño*, has been universally translated from the Castilian of Bernal Diaz Del Castillo into the English adjective of color "chestnut," *castanea*, the reader may find the listings of the colors of the horses brought by Cortez confusing and not in accordance with those of previous listings, or of the listings in other books of the reader's acquaintance. At the risk of contradicting myself, I would like to corect this discrepancy by explaining that Dr. Francisco Montaño D.V.M. of Sevilla, Spain, technical director of the sales, exportation and breeding of Spanish Andalusian horses, in my presence, called a horse of bay color, *castaño*, and called a horse of the color which in the United States we call chestnut, *alazan*.

Hernando De Soto, "the finest horseman of the Conquest," returned to Spain from the Conquest of Peru with Inca gold worth millions of dollars in today's money. He scoured Spain and Portugal for the best soldiers, the best horses and the best armaments to use on his expedition into what is now the southern United States. When he had selected the best, he sailed for Florida and landed there hoping to find another Montezuma or Atahualpa, another Mexico or Peru. He never found an ounce of gold. Instead he met some of the fiercest warriors on the North American continent. They fought with bows that could shoot an arrow through armor. The Indians harried him from Florida to the banks of the Mississippi, and there, no longer a conquistadore, but a fugitive, he died.

He had landed with one hundred and fifty of the finest horses in Europe and had lost most of them through hunger, fatigue, wounds and capture. His followers abandoned the few that remained to them and embarked down the river.

There had been horses in Florida since the time of Ponce De Leon (1460–1521) and the Indians had surely by the time of De Soto learned the value of the horse. It is logical to assume that they took the horses and used them.

The legend to the effect that the Indians of the southern states would never cross their horses with those of the English colonists of Virginia and Georgia may have some bearing on the matter. The fine horses abandoned on the banks of the Mississippi could very well have been the progenitors of the appaloosa of the Northwest, in view of the fact that early French explorers found Indians riding horses on the future site of St. Louis, in the 1600's. It is within the realm of possibility that descendants of De Soto's horses fell into the hands of the Pawnee horsetraders who spread the Spanish horse into the far Northwest.

Although the Spaniards claimed that the Indians fled from the tame horses that were turned loose in Florida, later studies have proved that the Spaniards exaggerated in many of their statements. It is ridiculous to think that, expert naturalists that they were, the Indians could not have recognized a valuable animal when they saw one. Even in the first major battle with Indians, Cortez lost two horses. The Indians killed them to prove that they were mortal. The proof that Indians got possession of horses immediately after the arrival of the Spaniards is that the Indians used *La Jineta* methods in their riding, methods which the first Spaniards brought from Spain and discarded soon after their arrival in the New World.

The Indians took the best and strongest horses from the Spaniards because tame animals could seldom survive or resist the attacks of predators in severe desert or frigid climates such as Nevada, Utah or Wyoming. Vaqueros who drove across those states say that cattle which became foot-sore, exhausted or hurt and dropped out of a herd always became a prey to wolves or coyotes. Whenever vaqueros backtracked a beef that had dropped behind they found trampled places which showed where the beef had stopped to fight off the predators; but they were always pulled down. When the vacqueros got there, all they would find would be gnawed bones. However, this did not hold true with horses, nor did it always happen with cattle. Strong, well nourished animals turned out on the range could protect themselves and soon learned to fight off their enemies and propagate themselves.

The first Andalusian horses in America were of many colors. There were buckskins, pintos, palominos and very likely an appaloosa among the first arrivals. Diaz speaks of "the good pied mare of Juan De Salamanca." Juan was riding the mare on the day that he killed a *cacique* (chief) and saved the day for the Spaniards.

The Spanish horse came to California through Durango to Sonora with the forces of Diego De Ibarra who brought sixty Basques and many Indian auxiliaries from Durango to conquer the Mayo Indians. Martinez De Urdaide, another Basque, "the strong right arm of the Jesuit Company" later brought more horses into what is now Sonora. From there horses were crossed into Baja California and still later into Alta California.

The Andalusian horse's greatest contribution to man, however, was not the help he gave in winning battles against Indians, but the progeny he left in the New World, the *criollos* of South America and the mustangs of North America. Faithful unto death to both the white man and the redman, they charged as tirelessly and magnificently into a forest of obsidian-tipped Aztec spears for their Spanish masters as they raced into a herd of stampeding buffalo for their Indian masters. Utterly loyal, they were the perfect horses for the task of moving the millions of head of cattle which they spread over two continents from the Straits of Magallanes to the Arctic Circle, over mountains and across prairie and desert, from the Atlantic to the Pacific and beyond. They were cherished by *gaucho, huaso, charro, vaquero, buckaroo* and the *paniola* of the far Hawaiian Islands.

Although the criollo and mustang in reverting to the feral state never retained the classic beauty of their European forebears, by being forged in the inclement elements of desert, prairie and mountain, in extremes of heat and cold and variations of feed and water, they became even more enduring than their famed Andalusian forebears, the greatest warhorses in Europe.

Of the countless thousands of wild horses that roamed the plains and deserts of California, the best were found in the Valley of the Tulares (San Joaquin). Even though the San Joaquin Valley was already being settled in 1849, there were numerous horses ranging over it. The native Californians constructed long wings of willow brush which converged into a corral into which they drove the horses and caught them with their *lazos*. But the numbers of mustangs did not decrease perceptibly until years later. With the advent of the mobs of miners who came in the Gold Rush, horses which had once been slaughtered and driven over cliffs to cut down on their numbers, suddenly became valuable. The vaqueros began hunting them extensively and corraling them in enormous herds, catching as many as five hundred in one day. The hunters selected the best horses in the herds, killing or leaving the rest. For years afterwards the bones of the thousands killed in the chase lay bleaching on the plains.

True Spanish mustangs survived in some parts of California until well into the present century and were found on the Carriso Plains as late as 1910. The horses on the Carriso were of a pure Spanish strain, as were the Barileño horses of the Mojave, and distinct from the degenerate broomtails found in some other parts of the West. The difference in wild horses was that the true mustang never degenerated in the wild state as did the broomtails.

I remember a little pin-eared, ram-headed gray mustang in San Luis Obispo County—he looked like the horses in George Catlin's drawings—one of the last to run on the Carriso Plains. He was a perfect little piece of horse flesh, though he did not weigh over six hundred pounds, soaking wet. In quality he compared very favorably with the Andalusian horses I saw in Spain—the Portuguese dressage horses could have been his brothers—and looked just like the little bouncing Barbs I saw in the vicinity of Rabat, Morocco. He never lost his wild instincts, however, and remained a wild horse to the last and never learned to trust mankind. He never failed to whistle a warning and snort loudly when anyone approached, and if he ever got loose it would take hours to run him down and catch him.

As late as the 1920's feral horses still ran in the Sierra around Breckenridge and in the desert along the eastern base of the Sierra Nevada. But they were not true mustangs. There are still horses that are called "wild" in Antelope Valley, once the home of the famed Barileño mustang; but they are horses descended from an Arabian stallion Rawley Duntley obtained from the Tejon Ranch some years ago. The true mustang is gone forever.

Several times in his history the Andalusian horse has been all but destroyed as a breed. First by kings who brought Germanic horses into Spain and crossed them with the native stock, and then by the French who took the Spanish horses as spoils of war. But each time, patriotic Spaniards have gathered the remnants of their despoiled studs and began again to perpetuate their native breed of pure-blooded horses.

The Andalusian horse was dealt its worst blow during the reign of Felipe III who handed over the direction of the royal stud to an Italian, Geronimo Tituli. This man crossed *"el magnifico caballo Andaluz"* with the "ram-headed German beasts." His purpose was to produce horses for heavy cavalry, a type which could compare with the medieval charger, the *dextrarius* (destrier), that was led by a page while its master rode to the tournament or battlefield astride a pacing jennet or palfrey.

Fortunately for future horsemen, certain breeders would not cross their beautiful mares with the foreign stallions, but kept their blood unsullied. These breeders deserve to have their names in bronze. They were Picado, Zamora, Calero, Carrero, Retemales, Guzman, Valenzuela and the monks of the religious order of Carthusians who were famous as trainers of warhorses. The Andalusian horse has often been called "Carthusian," "monks" or "monastery" horse, because the monks of that order were the trainers and breeders. This complicated training which is perpetuated in the Spanish Riding School of Lippiza was not completed until the animal's seventh year, that is after four years of training. The Portuguese who train horses for the bull ring still take four years to complete a horse's schooling.

The Andalusian is still the world's great dressage horse, and is at his magnificent best performing in the Portuguese style of bull fighting, *Toreo A La Jineta*, or *Rejoneo* under another of its names since there are several schools of this style of bullfighting. The Portuguese *Festa Dos Touros* is an elaborate ceremony with many historical overtones.

After the prohibition of tournaments and duels in the Peninsula, the nobles began fighting bulls on horseback for the purpose of improving their military skill. However, the tradition goes back two thousand years. The Greek historian, Strabo, said, "The horsemen inhabiting the coastal regions of the Peninsula like to challenge isolated bulls which in Hispania are very wild."

The fighters, dressed in eighteenth century fashion, arrive at the arena in a decorated coach preceded by heralds and standard bearers. The *cavalieros* mount their horses in the arena and begin the *festa* by showing off their horses in the graceful, intricate figures and patterns of the *Haute Ecole*.

The bullfight, however, has its tense moments. To begin with, the horseman must await the bull's charges face to face, and the darts must be placed in the bull's neck with a downward thrust, but not until the bull's horns are touching the rider's stirrup. Moreover, the *cavaliero* must never move the horse until the bull charges, and finally, he must not place the horse in a position where he may be hurt. However, the horse is seldom hurt since he is carefully and superbly trained over a period of time in which he reaches near perfection.

Throughout their colthood Spanish horses are left to run in the pastures with the fighting bull calves, and thus learn that bulls are dangerous and to be wary of them. Over the long period of their training the horses are used on the breeding farms to work cattle, to pursue, test and overthrow cows and young bulls. In their contests with the bulls, the horses learn that the bull indicates each movement by the look or the movement of his ears, and the horses know even before their riders do when a bull will be wild or difficult. The horses are so highly trained and so sensitive that on the mornings of the bull fight, the moment the rider enters the stable, the horses will indicate by their actions that they know they will face fighting bulls that afternoon.

The various strains of Andalusian are named after the breeders who founded them, and all have a legend of a founding sire that had once belonged to an emperor, caliph or sultan, and had been found pulling a cart or carrying a pack or doing some other ignoble task when his quality was recognized and he was bought for a song. All these legends seem to have a common origin and parallel that of the Godolphin Barb. The original Guzman was owned by a peddler who sold him to a breeder for small change.

The farrier, Andres Zamora, after whom the Zamorano strain of Andalusians is named, saw a blue-gray horse carrying a load of treelimbs used to fire ovens. He bought him on the spot for 20 *escudos* and took him to his small ranch where he turned him out with the mares. In time the old horse sired a "blue-gray colt with black points, very tight in the arms and thighs." When the colt was two years old his fame had spread so that a trader came all the way from Portugal to offer 4000 pesos in Portuguese gold doubloons for him. Our chronicler observes: "We can imagine the sweet ring of the Portuguese gold on Zamora's little ranch." Taking the joy from this, however, is the reported tale that the colt had been sold to the trader by a brother of Andres Zamora when Andres was at Sevilla; he returned and found the colt gone and despite the pile of Portuguese gold, he was so mortified that he took to his bed and never rose from it again.

It was not until dressage or *Haute Ecole* became the rage in Europe and Germanic horses began to be trained in that school, that "Spanish" bits (which were actually Neapolitan) came into use in the Kingdom of Naples. Bits were complicated mouthpieces and ports, serrated steel nosebands, were invented to be used on the cross bred horses that did not have the temperament for the *Haute Ecole* training. Rusio, Fiaschi, Corte and Pignatelli were some of the more famous masters of the Italian school.

The severity practiced in this school was not acceptable to Spaniards because the pure bred Andalusian did not need severity. He was fitted by breeding and temperament for complicated schooling and could be taught the *passage, pasada, posata, levada, corveta, lalotada* and *capriola* with the mildest of bits. Because the Andalusian horses were easier to train, and the system of schooling was much less intricate, the books written on the training of horses (La Jineta) by Spaniards and Portuguese were much easier to understand.

In spite of the fact that it is offensive to the Spanish people and to scholars who have made a thorough study of the ages-old Iberian hippology, self-proclaimed authorities persist in writing that the Andalusian horse is an "Arabian," and that the horses brought to the Americas by *conquistadores* were also blue-blooded "Arabians." No statement was ever made on thinner evidence. One old windbag writes, "These breeds (Kehilian Arabs) were poured into Spain by the thousands by the Moors." Even Moorish historians deny this, and emphatically state the opposite!

These writers ignore the fact that Spaniards were breeding horses centuries before the Moslem invasion of Europe, that numerous bands of Tarpan-like horses roamed the plains of Europe and were the chief article of diet of primitive Spaniards. Long before the dawn of history Iberians had stopped hunting the horse for food. They had fashioned a bit of staghorn or bronze, and started riding the wild horses, though they were no bigger than modern burros. The Spanish horse was famous for his speed and quality a thousand years before Taric El Tuerto led his forces into Spain, and the Andalusian has been a fine horse for as many centuries as the Arabian.

The Duke of Newcastle, one of the greatest horsemen of his age, says of the Andalusian, "Absolutely the best stallions in the world to breed horses for war and running races." He persuaded Charles II to import them in great numbers. They were still in great demand in England for the reception of William III for Household Cavalry and parade horses.

The American-Spanish horse or mustang gives proof of his color. The dun or slate color with dorsal stripe, the roan color and the ramhead are Tarpan-like characteristics common to the feral horse of the Americas.

It is preposterous to state, as some writers do, that the men who made up the rank and file of the Moslem cavalry—Egyptians, Sudanese, Abyssinians, Persians, Libyans, Algerians, Tunisians, Moors and all the others of the motley races of North Africa that swept across the North African littoral and invaded Spain—were riding fine Arabian steeds when Arabia was hardly a horse-breeding country. Modern pictures of Sudanese, Abyssinians, Moors and others show them riding good Barb-type horses, but these horses are far from being Arabians as we know them.

The horses brought by Vandals and other Norsemen could have had as much influence on the Andalusian as the Barb since the Isabella color (yellow) with head "bending like a hawk's beak" is common in both Scandinavian and Iberian horses. The Arabian reproduces himself with astonishing uniformity and horses that have Arabian blood, no matter what other bloods they may have, never fail to show it. As an example: the Lippizan was outcrossed with the Arabian, and after three hundred years of breeding, often shows Arabian characteristics. True, the Andalusian resembles the little Moroccan Barb more than he does any other horse, but for that matter, the thoroughbred resembles the Andalusian much more than he does the Arabian, and if the truth were told the thoroughbred owes as much, or more, to the Spanish mares that were imported to England than he does to the Arabian. The Arabian has made much horse history. He is a fine animal; but before giving the Arabian credit for everything we should remember that there were other horses that were just as good or even better. Spaniards were riding horses centuries before an Arab ever rode a horse. Fine Libyan horses, bays with black points, were famous throughout the Roman Empire long before the time of Christ.

Bundville described the Spanish jennets thus: Finely made,

very seemly to the eye, in swiftness they surpass all horses that be, even as the eagle surpasses all the birds of the air. "They have carried their riders out of the battle field I cannot tell how many miles after the jennets have been shot through the body with arquebuses, which report I have heard to be true by divers of own soldiers."

Chapter 3

INDIAN HORSES

Although the Spaniards brought the first horses to America, it is to the Indian that we are indebted for spreading the herds of wild horses over two continents. The Indians saw the value of the horse the moment the first Andalusian stallion set foot on the shores of the New World, and from that moment the struggle for possession of the animals began between Spaniards and Indians, and did not end for centuries. The Spaniards fought to keep horses out of the hands of the Indians and enacted the Law of the Indies which forbade Indians the use of the horse. The Indians fought the law and exerted every effort to secure the animals.

It was a struggle the Indians won, and the proof lies in the thousands of wild horses in both North and South America which existed where the white man had never set foot. Indeed, if the Anglo-Saxon had stayed out of the North American West, the Indians in time would have wreaked their revenge on the murderers of Cuauhtemoctzin. In another century the Indians would have driven the Spaniards out of much of North America.

It is reasonable to suppose that the Indians tried to scatter the Spaniards' horses as much to deprive them of their most formidable weapon of offense as to acquire a means of transportation for themselves. Anyone with much less perception than an Indian, made desperate by cruelty and the threat of slavery, could have seen how helpless the heavily armored Spaniards would be without their horses. As early as 1554 the

Indians near Zacatecas were taking horses and driving them north toward the vast plains which begin in the neighboring state of Durago and spread north across Chihuahua into the limitless prairies of North America to the rim of the Arctic Circle, a whole continent in which horses could run free and multiply.

The horse changed the Western Indian from a skulking creature groping his way on foot across the vast expanse of the continent, subsisting on rodents, reptiles and roots, to a horseman and warrior. The mustang brought the Kiowa and Comanche out of the deserts of the Great Basin to the Plains to feast on the meat of the buffalo. It was the horse that made it possible for the Apache to raid from the high deserts of Arizona for five hundred miles south into the tablelands of Mexico, and ironically, the horse that ("after God") had won the conquest for the Spaniards, when mounted by Apache, Comanche and Navajo, stopped Spanish territorial expansion in Western North America.

The Spanish horse of California brought Blackfoot, Shoshone and Piute across the Sierra Nevada into the lush pastures along the coast to raid the missions and ranches. Mustangs were driven in many thousands over the Cajon, Tejon, Tehachapi, Walker's and other passes into New Mexico and across the Great Basin and over the Rockies into the prairie states.

Although they have been eulogized by the writers of apocryphal histories of California, the furtive "trappers" who lurked in the Great Basin during the first half of the last century and cohabited with Indian women, were more often than not scalp hunters whose hands were stained with the blood of inoffensive Indians (the Diggers) who were slaughtered for the price on scalps. They encouraged the Utes to raid the mission ranches on the coast of California, corrupted them with rot-gut whiskey and cheated them out of their hard won spoils. Nor did those "trappers" scruple against cannibalism when pressed by hunger in the long northern winters. Misinformers of humanity write in praise of these men (Carson, for one) who shot down defenseless children (the De Haro boys) in cold blood; and, without a trace of irony, call them heroes.

It was the constant menace of hostile Indians and fear of them that often prevented the Spaniards from gathering horses that strayed into Indian territory and caused them to abandon animals which reverted to the wild state.

The Indians in California learned much from the Spaniards, and learned it fast. In following the Spaniards' maxim, *Cien años de perdon a el que roba un ladron* (one hundred years of pardon for one who robs a robber), the Indians set about accruing a few indulgences for themselves. Very early in the history of ranching in California the problem of Indians running off horses from the missions and ranches assumed serious proportions.

The first Indian recorded to have taken horses away from the Spaniards was Jorge, no doubt an unwilling neophyte who had lingered around one of the missions long enough to learn to ride and to covet a horse. He set so good an example for his fellow tribesmen that in over a period of twenty years, it has been estimated, a hundred thousand head of horses were taken from the missions of Santa Cruz, San Jose and Monterey, as well as from private ranches. The Indians were often pursued and many were killed in the running fights, but they were very bold, and it was not until E. F. Beale, "the lord of all he surveyed," brought soldiers to Fort Tejon, that large-scale raiding was brought to a stop. However, the Indians kept the Spaniards from developing the San Joaquin through the period of raiding.

Of course, the Indians were not altogether free from the "help" of the Anglos. The "trappers," most of them scalp hunters, lurked in the Great Basin east of the Sierra Nevada and waited for the Indians to drive the horses over the mountains. They went back east with many head of horses.

In 1846 a group of men coming to aid the taking over of

California for the United States met a "Captain Walker" and ten drovers driving east with a band of "five hundred of the best horses in California."

As early as 1850 considerable traffic in livestock was going on in the Great Basin; Mormons, immigrants, goldseekers, scalp hunters and Indians were trafficking in horses, cattle and equipment. From the advent of Mormons in Utah until the building of the railroads, the livestock industry of Nevada and Utah was interlaced with that of California. California horses known as "Spanish horses"—to distinguish them from the horses brought from the East and the Indian horses—"because they had no end of bottom" were much sought after to ride in the running fights between the pioneers and the Tima-Utes, Yampa-Utes and Pi-Utes who united to fight against the whites.

Sometimes the horse ran his heart out for his rider in trying to overtake a fleeing Indian; at other times, with the circumstances reversed, he raced to save his rider from a band of pursuing Indians. The races were always close because the Indians' horses had been taken from the Mission herds of the Coast. The only thing in the white man's favor was that he had selected and bought the best of the horses bred in California and fed them grain.

An official of the Mormon Church wrote about that period: "In California we bought fine Spanish horses and mules, bought good riding saddles, and set out for Salt Lake which we reached in twenty-one days. We had the best horses in the territory. On the Humbolt River we met a heavy migration going to California, this (1852) being the heaviest year for immigrants. With the immigrants going West I traded lame or tired stock and paid five dollars for good animals, seldom over. I bought Durhams which were heavy and tender and could not be driven through. From these animals I raised and had premium stock at the Salt Lake fairs for many years afterward. I also traded with the California drovers and bought animals for less than half of what they were worth. Drover after drover passed daily, most of which had lame or tired animals to sell."

He says this of a skirmish with the Indians: "We were chased by this band of Utes. The Indians put their ponies down to their best. We outran them for a while, then we held our own. But one Indian, riding a spotted horse, came on ahead of the rest at full speed. I wanted that pony. He was as pretty as a speckled bird. But I was in too much of a hurry. The other Indians were too close; I had to pull away, so my horse carried me off at lightning speed."

CHAPTER 4

OLD TIMERS AND SUCH

A rusty bridle bit, a broken spur, a few scraps of a fading tradition are all that remain of a classic horsemanship that thrived for a hundred and fifty years in California.

Gone are the rancheros, the grave, bearded men of Arab dignity whose stately gestures were as eloquent as their clipped, archaic Castilian; gone are the youths who rode out into the wilds to capture the truculent grizzly bear with rawhide ropes; gone are the girls with the soft, brown Moorish eyes who danced whole days and nights with a tireless vitality; gone are the musicians who strummed guitars through days and nights of fiesta; gone are the gentle Indian retainers who were to meet injustice with dignity.

Gone are the great ranchos with their broad acres and sprawling, flatroofed adobe houses, where the stranger was welcome to stay for a day or for a lifetime; gone are the cactus hedges which enclosed the apricots, figs, olives, grapes and pomegranates which Semites had brought to Spain from some far Eastern land, and which dedicated priests had guarded across stormy seas and burning deserts to plant in California.

Gone are the numerous droves of wild Andalusian horses; gone are the fierce, brindled Spanish bulls that were a match for any predator that dared attack them; gone are the rodeos with their thousands of milling, bawling, wild-eyed cattle, held in check by eager, gallant little mustangs; gone are the vaqueros with their silver-inlaid bits and spurs, their buttoned, braided reins and remals, their beautiful, tooled-leathered saddles on which were always strapped the ever ready reatas that held death in their sinuous loops.

I met him on one of those mornings which could come only to the Southern California of fifty years ago. It was late February after a rain. The sun was warm and all the world was green, with a carpet of grass spreading kneedeep over the Rosa De Castilla Hills that rim the San Gabriel Valley. The orange trees were in bloom, and the fragrance of *azahar*, so loved by the Moors of Spain, hung in heavy drowsy air. The green of the trees melting into the darker shades of the Sierra Madres, capped with snow on the higher peaks in the background, unrolled a panorama of the Southern California I knew in my boyhood and shall always love and remember.

He came riding through the *alfileria*, sitting erect in his high-horned saddle, his reins nipped delicately in the fingers of his left hand, and I knew him to be an *hijo del pais* (son of the country). He was an old man. His bearded face was seamed and weatherbeaten, yet it had that touch of grace common to the old Californianos.

He rode one of the finest horses I had ever seen—a bright, blood bay with black points, and not a single white hair on his body; even his hoofs were black. Young as I was and as little as I knew about horses, I could recognize his quality as the old man rode up and stopped beside me.

Fifty years ago there were still a few of the old horsemen left. Nicolas Covarrubias, Mariscal Lugo, Jose Ibarra—who now belong to legend, riders of a bygone era who lived with the herds of long gone Spanish cattle, droves of mustangs and the vaqueros who had ridden into oblivion a half century before. He greeted me in that half-mocking tone all old men of that period used when they spoke to kids.

"*¿Ah, vagamundo, para donde vas?*" (Ah, vagabond, where are you going?) I had sense enough to acknowledge kinship in respect for his gray hairs.

"*Tio, vine a verlo trabajar su caballo.*" (Uncle, I came to see you work your horse.)

The old man smiled.

The horse was standing perfectly still; only his ears moved back and forth. The old man moved his feet. The spur chain rattled against the metal bottom of the stirrup. The horse was instantly alert. His ears turned back, the better to catch any signal from his rider. The old man raised his reins and twisted his wrist ever so slightly. The horse spun to the left. The old man twisted his wrist in the opposite direction. The horse spun to the right. The old man raised his reins and shook them. The horse trotted backwards. Suddenly the old man leaned forward, and instantly the horse sprang forward and stopped when the old man dropped the reins on his neck. The old man walked the horse two hundred paces away from me and turned him around toward me. He stood for a moment, then he tightened his reins and leaned forward. The horse leaped into a fast run. When he was abreast of me, the old man squeezed his legs, and raised the hand which held the reins; but he did not pull. The horse came to a sliding stop. If the old man had been carrying a glass of water, he would not have spilled a drop.

I was reminded of the stories my grandmother had told of riders racing to bring her a glass of wine, and stopping their horses with a tray of glasses in their hands without spilling a drop, at the *fiestas* in Los Angeles a century ago when she and California had been young together, and she had danced the *varsoviana* with Don Andres and Don Pio Pico.

Here was a perfect affinity, a horse in accord with his master. It is said that when a person wishes hard, he prays. If that is true, then I prayed; for I wished very hard to be able some day to ride and handle a horse as that old man could. With the reins hanging loose, he had used his body and legs to move that horse smoothly, rhythmically, and beautifully.

On that day I became the shadow of Andres Palomino. Palomino is an old Castilian surname, and, in this case had nothing to do with the adjective denoting color which is applied to a yellow horse, and is derived from the noun *paloma* (dove).

He would mount me on one of his horses, and as I rode

beside him he would give me terse counsel on handling horses; and these are some of the spare, pointed rules which he set forth in the short time I sat at his feet, so to speak, and learned about horses. I have remembered much of what he told me because, even then, I catalogued in my memory everything I was told about horses.

"Our Moorish-Andalusian ancestors left us a heritage of horsemanship which all *hijos del pais* foster and hold dear. Our way of riding is still the art of those ancient *jinetes*, the shifting of the weight, the pressure of the knees, the placing of the spur against the horse's side to establish communication between horse and rider, which we call *ayudas* (aids). If you signal your horse by using the aids, you will not have to pull continuously on your horse's mouth and your horse will not become hard from the constant pulling. His mouth as a result will remain responsive.

"Teach your horse to stop early in the morning rather than late in the afternoon. A horse worked in the afternoon will not dry out. Most cases of strangles result from a horse passing the night with a wet coat. Besides, in the early morning the sun's rays are horizontal, and if a man is not sensitive enough in the seat of his pants to feel by the horse's movements when his horse's feet are in the right position for the pull, then the rider can watch his shadow so he can see the position of the horse's legs, and pull him to a sliding stop."

One morning I arrived as he was saddling a young horse. I watched him pull the cinch up tight.

"It is better to cure whatever sores a horse may get than to mend broken bones when the saddle turns because of a loose cinch. Besides, a broken neck can never be mended."

He led the horse around in a small circle for a few turns. This practice is called *"Tres pasos de la muerte"* (Three paces of death). Vaqueros do this to avoid being hurt in the event a horse is a cinchbinder (falls over backwards when cinched tightly).

"It is better for the horse to fall with the empty saddle. That way he will only break the cantle, and that is better than for him to break the rider's neck.

"It is hard to put a rein on a horse without cattle. With cattle the horse does not always have his mind on his rider, and has a purpose in turning and stopping. After he has learned to turn after a cow he will associate the laying of the rein on his neck with turning, and besides, the work takes the fine edge off a colt.

"See that the knot on the *jaquima* is tied so that it won't loosen. A knot that works loose when the colt is pulled causes him to pull or lug on the *jaquima*.

"Do not ride a colt in the *jaquima* too long without putting a bit in his mouth, or he will become habituated to the *jaquima*, and, as a result, will become hard to accustom to the bit. Most luggers are made that way.

"Do not tie the rein of the *jaquima* to the saddle to give the colt a headset. Doing that will only teach him to lay against it, and he will lose all feeling around his nose.

"Do not pull a colt with both reins of the *jaquima* to stop him. Pull by doubling him with one rein. *And do not pull a colt more than once a day.*

"There is no such thing as a stupid horse; there are only stupid riders; and if a man says his horse is no good, it is because the man is no good.

"In riding horses one must remember that the art of reining horses is centuries old, that only the purpose, not the method, has changed, that the use of bits was established by exact laws and principles of mechanics that have proved accurate since the Moors brought the art of riding *A La Jineta* into Spain, that good reinsmen are always old men, that there is no substitute for patience in teaching a horse; that if a horse doesn't do as his rider wishes it is because the horse doesn't understand his rider.

"Never put a bit without a port in your horse's mouth. A

horse cannot keep his tongue in place with a bit that has no port, because the tongue is always slipping over the mouthpiece and letting it rest on the bars and bruising them."

The vaquero of California inherited the science of *La Jineta* and adopted it to the working of cattle and the lassoing of grizzly bears, buffalo, elk, and any other animal that he met in the course of his riding. The sliding stop, the spin to the right or to the left, and the trot backwards, the *testerazo* (the blow with the horse) were retained, while the uses of warfare, such as the *capriole*, in the execution of which the horse leaps into the air and kicks to rid himself of clinging enemies, while very useful to the Spaniards when Aztec warriors swarmed around them, were discarded when the soldiers settled on the ranches to raise cattle; but at heart the old soldiers remained cavalrymen.

However, after a period of time in working cattle all horses worked independently of their rider. In fact, the best reined horses were the best working cattle horses and would follow a beef through a herd of thousands and never lose it, without the rider once lifting his hand to guide his horse. The instinct for working cattle was called *amor al ganado* ("cow sense" by the gringos). If a horse had the intelligence to take a good rein it followed that he had the intelligence to work cattle, play polo, or show in a stock horse class. As a matter of fact, Marco Hellman, one of the first men to consistently show stock horses in the show ring in California, combed the ranches and bought the best horses that had been trained with cattle, to show in stock horse classes.

There was a little sorrel Nevada horse on Pimentel Ranch on the Carrizo Plains. He would get behind a cow in the middle of a herd of thousands of cattle, lay his ears back, and drive it out of the herd. If the cow didn't move fast enough he would bite it on the tail. He was never known to have let a cow get away from him. Juan Reyes who worked for Burt Snedden liked to see the little horse work. He would sit his horse on the outside of the herd and watch the little mustang.

He would laugh uproariously and say, "That little horse must be able to smell a Miller cow!"

As we have said, the vaquero was forever seeking a way to improve his skills and those of his horse. Putting the horse behind a cow, that is to say, working the horse with cattle, allowed the horse to teach himself. But this practice had its limitations. Although the horse soon took a rudimentary rein and learned to follow and turn a cow and drive it out of the herd without the guidance of its rider, this did not make for the trigger-reined horse which was the delight of the vaquero. For this reason the vaquero invented games in which to work his horse and improve its rein.

Vaqueros often played *Once* (Eleven). In this game a number of vaqueros would take turns racing their horses for a fixed distance and pulling them to a sliding stop. The purpose was to make two long, deep lines from the sliding hooves. These lines made a figure eleven. The longest *once*, or figure eleven, would decide the winner.

Although he was known far and wide on the ranches of the San Joaquin as a fancy roper, Guadalupe Ortiz introduced a game to the Miller and Lux vaqueros which was described in a horse magazine some years ago by a man who had once been a buckaroo on the Miller chuck wagon. This game was still being practiced by the chuck wagon crew on the Buttonwillow Ranch when Miller and Lux went out of business in 1927, years after 'Lupe had gone North to ride on other ranches. Whenever a vaquero or buckaroo would brag overmuch about his horse, two other riders would challenge him to a reining contest. In this game the three vaqueros would part out a yearling, preferably an active one, and drive it up to a fence and hold it there. The three riders would place themselves at an equal distance from each other along the fence. Then the rider on one end would try to drive the calf between the man in the middle and the fence. If he succeeded, the man on the other end would try to drive the calf back; and with the calf trying to break to the herd, there would be more than enough turning and spinning in which to teach a horse, besides showing the worth of the animal.

The vaquero took great pride in the horse that backed in a straight line at high speed, and few, indeed, were the vaquero horses that would not trot backwards. The horses acquired this proficiency because of the vaquero's practice of jumping his horse forward at the instant he wanted the animal to stop backing. This was simple deduction. The vaquero believed that since the horse exerted more effort in gathering himself and jumping forward than in backing, he would back rapidly to avoid jumping forward.

A horse that did not slide when he stopped was worthless in the vaquero's eyes. If a horse did not slide, he could not turn at a fast speed, so it behooved the vaquero to take pains in teaching him. The time-proven method of teaching a horse to stop properly was to be careful to pull him when his forehand was leaving the ground and his hind legs were well under him. In doing this, the vaquero did not assert a long, steady pull, nor pull both reins of the *jaquima*. He pulled one rein and made a series of short, quick pulls. A long, steady pull would tempt the horse to brace against the *jaquima*.

Men who spent years going from ranch to ranch, hunting polo pony prospects, say that many good horses were found on the big ranches. A horse that had speed, a little quality, and a good mouth never failed to interest a polo man. Since it is a well known fact that a horse with a trigger rein, to a large extent, worked cattle without the guidance of his rider, a buyer could never tell whether a good vaquero horse that was well reined and worked cattle perfectly, would play polo consistently.

A polo pony is ridden into scrimmages that are unknown to a vaquero horse, and takes a mauling which even the most patient vaquero horse would never submit to. Therefore, unless the horse was played on a polo field over a period of months, the buyer never knew whether a horse would shy away from a mallet stroke or from a horse that tried to ride him away from a ball.

Besides his other handicaps, the polo pony worked with a dry mouth. The bits used on polo ponies, unlike those used by vaqueros, were not made of steel, but of a metal which promoted dryness in the horse's mouth. They did not have the copper which sweetens and promotes moisture.

For the past twenty years this author has been opening and examining the mouths of many kinds of horses—show horses, rodeo and roping horses, jumping horses, polo horses—and has found that of the mouths cut up by pressures of the bit, those of polo horses were cut up the most. The roping horses, especially those ridden with leverage bits with snaffle mouthpieces, often had their tongues cut.

When trying out a polo prospect the hopeful buyer never failed to work the horse strenuously for a long period at high speed in figure eights, in circles, in runs-and-stops. He did this to see if the horse could stand the pressure and mauling of a seven-minute chukker. A pony that will respond to every demand of his rider in the melee of a hotly contested game of polo is a pearl beyond price and extremely hard to find.

Top left: antique spur; *top right* shows how the S-shank "US" bit can put a pressure of forty pounds on the horse's chin with a pull of only six pounds on the reins. *At center:* diagram shows how the leverage on a spade bit is less than that on an S-shank bit. *At right* is the spike spur. *At bottom:* A Sonora spur.

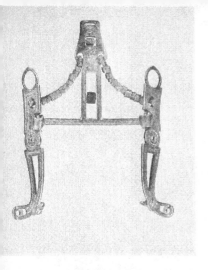
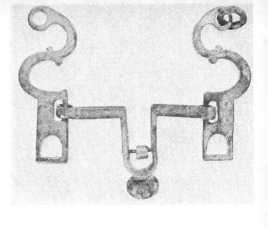

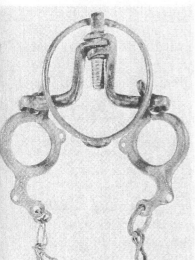
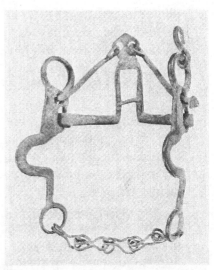

Top left: Barroyecca bit; *at right* is standard square bit. *At center: left,* is a hinged mouthpiece ringed bit; *at right* is a well worn antique home made bit of the last century. *Below left:* Crude spade bit dug up in the ruins of Barroyecca, destroyed by the Yaquis in 1700. *At right* can be seen the brand of the Terry Merello family, breeders of Andalusian horses. The C at center of brand identifies the famed Carthusian strain in this Andalusian.

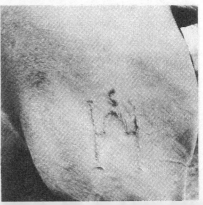

CHAPTER 5

THE BROWN VAQUERO HORSE

The sayings, proverbs and maxims which are woven into the fabric of California legends and folklore were so much a part of the vaquero's daily life that he applied them in all his dealings with men, horses, cattle and other denizens of the ranches. They were so often pat to the occasion or circumstance that he accepted them as the true experiences of life, and gained more from them than from the long poring-over of books.

When a vaquero saw a boy riding a young horse, he would say, "There goes a pair of dolts."

He meant that the boy didn't have experience enough to teach the horse, and that, as a result, the horse would never learn anything.

To a vaquero a horse was an open book in which his rider's virtues and vices were written for all to read. He could tell if a horse had had a young or an older rider. A horse ridden by an old man was always quiet, because old men never quarrel with their horses. A young man, on the other hand, will often fight his horse.

A horse that carried his head high, with his eyes rolled back, indicated that he had been jerked; a horse that jumped whenever his rider moved had been whipped; a horse that jerked his head away when his rider raised the bridle to put the bit in his mouth indicated that he had been hit over the head. A horse that reared or plunged had had too much spinning and turning and gone sour.

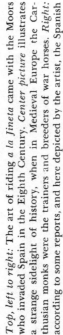

Top, left to right: The art of riding *a la Jineta* came with the Moors who invaded Spain in the Eighth Century. *Center picture* illustrates a strange sidelight of history, when in Medieval Europe the Carthusian monks were the trainers and breeders of war horses. *Right:* according to some reports, and here depicted by the artist, the Spanish Padres of the New World sometimes went to great lengths to get neophytes. *Below, left to right:* three moments of high excitement captured by the artists Badilla and Barreto. We see two ways of capturing a bronco and at center, the artist says, "They smelled water."

Charlie Hitchcock, *top left*, and George Brunk, *bottom left*, leave nothing unsaid in these fine photos. Brunk was foreman of the San Emideo Ranch when photographed in the 1920's. The pen and ink studies show, *top*, a modern-day Baja California vaquero, and *below*, an idealized man-and-horse blending into one spirit of elegant action. The Baja Californian wears buckskin *cuerra* and *botas* that have not changed in style since they were introduced into California by the "leather jacket" soldiers of Spain in 1769.

Fifty years ago, the author with fifteen other riders bunked down in the upper story of the above "landmark" at Painted Rock on the Carriso Plains. The two vaqueros at *right,* Juan Reyes and Jim Stewart, preserved forever in this 1926 photo, were the sort to provide good company on any occasion on the plains. *Below* is a modern-day scene at Alamos, Sonora, as local ranchers show up in town for a holiday.

Above left, is a typical Charro—an amateur dedicated to preserving the ancient arts of horsemanship. Here we see a Charro demonstrating turning—an example of horse and rider trained to perfection. *At right* are two scenes showing how tailing is done. The steer is lifted off the ground before being suddenly released. Expert horsemanship is required just to keep the saddle from being turned and dumping the rider. *Below,* a Charro demonstrates the next-to-last action as the steer is about to be literally spun in mid-air. A complete fall with all four legs pointing skyward means the steer has been successfully tailed.

Left, above, our artist depicts what he calls "an unforseen event" on the range. But any rider worth his leather was always ready to react to a bucking horse *At right* is the recreation of an historical incident in the 1860's, when a certain McCoy sought out the biggest buffalo for display East of the Mississippi. He first had to find some vaqueros who could successfully rope a buffalo and tie him down. Apparently he succeeded. In the drawing *at right* we are shown how the last of the wild hogs along the Merced River were ridden down and caught in 1945. *Below:* Land Company and Miller and Lux vaqueros are seen engaged in one of their little-known side-lines. For obvious reasons, there was a strong market in elks' teeth, and our riders bore down on the magnificent Tule Elk to get the teeth.

The real West of long ago lives on in the two ponies shown here. *At top* is a little mustang, underfed and undersized, but as tough as whang leather. The mustang in the *lower photo* shows descent from Andalusian *tordas* (grays).

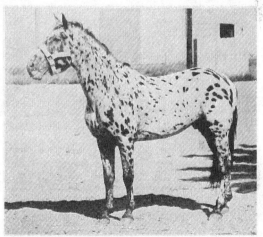

At top is Nevado, one of the finest of the Andalusian breed. Photo was taken at Jerez, Spain. *Above, right,* is an Andalusian appaloosa, bred by the Duchess of Alba and brought to Mexico by Tony Aguilar. *Seen below* are wild horses of Russia. They have zebra stripes typical of the tarpan-like horse.

The Portuguese school of horsemanship and bullfighting differs from the Spanish and Mexican. *At top and at bottom* two riders can be seen in full regalia. In Portugal the bull would not be killed, but when performing in Mexico or Spain, the fatal blow is dealt. *In the pen and ink sketch* we can see how the Portuguese horseman often drops his reins and depends on knee and leg pressure to manage his horse.

I discovered that a horse reflects the worth of his rider as soon as I began riding the brown horse Don Jesus Lopez gave me to ride in the rodeos on Tejon Ranch forty-five years ago. There I began to admire and know a man whom I was not to meet until months later, but whom I knew through the brown horse he had ridden.

The horse was of the color which we *Californianos* call *retinto*, that reddish-brown or sunburnt-black which occurs in horses of his breeding. Although it was obvious that standard bred blood predominated in his ancestry, a strain of coach-horse blood could be discerned in his stout shoulders and legs. He was not a pretty horse, yet he was by no means an ugly one. His quality compared very favorably with that of the horses of thoroughbred Arabian breeding on Tejon Ranch. He had the large fine eyes and the lean ram-head which, from time immemorial, men who have timed and ridden horses have learned to associate with intelligence and courage; and the long angular body which is conducive to that stride which covers mile after weary mile, from sunup to sunset, day after day on the roundup and gives the lie to the belief that a horse must be "short-coupled" to be good.

He was the best horse I have ever ridden in the fifty-odd years of a life that has been a series of different horses. He taught me to work cattle, and to know and appreciate a good vaquero, and I dare say, in the course of a useful life he taught other green boys how to work. He was at his best when the work of parting out beef for the buyer was in progress, and he and his rider had a position holding the herd. Without the guidance of his rider he would pace his position back and forth between the horse and rider stationed on each side of him, with his head turned toward the herd and his ears pricked forward, ready for any steer that should break out of the herd. He seemed to know when a steer intended to make a dash for freedom. The moment the steer broke, the brown horse would be after him. He would race up beside him and when the horse had his shoulder just past that of the steer, he would very gradually crowd the steer and force him to turn in a circle back to the herd. *Paisanos* call this method of turning back a beef *"pagarse a la paleta"* (closeup or crowded up to the shoulder). There was no violent stopping and spinning back on the haunches, no unnecessary wearing out of horseshoes or raising of dust, as in the method of cruder working vaquero horses. Here was the smooth, finished job of a master craftsman.

But turning a steer back to the herd smoothly and efficiently was not the brown horse's only virtue. Sometimes when his rider would be "visiting" with the rider stationed around the herd next to him, or dreaming of how he was going to spend his next month's wages, or was half asleep and not tending to his business, he would suddenly be jolted back into wakefulness when the horse would leap out after a steer. After a young vaquero got a few jolts or falls by way of education, he would stay awake as long as he had the brown horse between his legs.

Because he was, as Don Jesus put it, *muy noble* (very gentle) he would be given some green kid who could learn from him. One day such a lad was riding the brown with the vaqueros on the rodeos in the mountains.

In a rodeo the vaqueros spread out in a circle, then back and converge on a central point, driving the cattle. The spot where the cattle are gathered is called the rodeo ground, and the act is called *parrar rodeo* (to hold rodeo). The *caporal*, or foreman, would point out a landmark, usually the top of a mountain, and order a vaquero to ride that far and bring back all the cattle he found on the way. Then he would send the next man to the top of the next ridge to bring back all the cattle on that ridge. This would go on until all the men were placed to cover a certain amount of territory. Because Tejon cattle were very wild, the *caporal* would pick two or three of the best men as *puestos,* men posted to stay on the ground to stop and hold the cattle as they poured down out of the mountains. It is a very important position; if the cattle are not stopped the whole day's work is wasted.

Don Toribio Cordova, the *caporal,* must have had some misgivings about the kid on the brown horse when he sent him up to the top of a mountain to bring down the cattle; but then the kid had to learn sometime.

He was told to stay in contact with the riders on each side of him in case one of them needed help or unseen cattle tried to escape or stay behind. Many calves were missed on the spring rodeos and an effort was always made to pick them up and brand them during the fall rodeos.

The kid climbed to the top of the ridge as he had been directed and turned back and began gathering cattle. He was halfway down when the brown horse espied a bunch of cows and calves escaping up a canyon away from the direction of the rodeo ground. Before his rider even caught sight of the strays, he leaped down the mountainside after them.

The bit the horse was wearing, being a cheap, light thing, only braced him so that he could run the better. He leaped over logs, through brush, and under trees, with the kid hanging on for dear life. On the way, just as the horse jumped over a log, a branch hit the kid and knocked him to the ground. Men who fall off horses are seldom seriously hurt, however. The kid picked himself up and limped down the mountain after the horse, which in this time, had disappeared after the cattle. The cattle, hearing the horse coming toward them, turned and joined a bunch going toward the rodeo ground and the brown continued after them until they joined the herd. The *puestos* were riding furiously around the herd milling them to prevent their escaping.

The riderless horse fell in behind one of the vaqueros and galloped round and round the herd until the rest of the men arrived and helped to bring the herd to a stop. One of the grinning vaqueros caught the brown and tied him to a tree to await his rider. Some time later the kid limped out of the brush to meet the grinning men.

"*¿Pero que paso con ese caballo hijo?* (But what happened with that horse, son?)" Don Jesus teased him.

I was only curious to know who had trained this horse to do things which I could only attribute to reasoning. I asked Don Toribio, the *caporal*, who had ridden the horse before me, and he answered, "*Es caballo lo andubo Adolfo Encinas* (That horse was ridden by Adolfo Encinas)."

"*A de ver sido muy buen vaquero* (He must have been a good vaquero,)" I said.

"*Si buen vaquero y buen lazador* (Yes, a good vaquero and a good lassoer)."

"*Y buen arrendador* (And a good reinsman,)" I suggested.

"*Si tenia mucha pacenia, y buen mano, y además si Adolfo anduviera en el caballo de su pior nemeigo, no lo estrujaba* (Ah, a great reinsman, with much patience and a good bridle hand. If Adolfo were to ride the horse of his worst enemy, he would never abuse the horse)."

"*¿Y el fue el que enseño este caballo?* (And he was the one who taught this horse?)"

"*No fue tanto que enseno el caballo sine que el dejo el caballo aprender. Todo caballo tiene inteligencia, lo que cuenta es dejarlo aprender* (It was not so much that he taught the horse, but that he let the horse learn. All horses have intelligence. Letting them learn is what counts)."

So I came to know a man through a good brown horse, and perhaps I might never have found a better way to learn a man's worth.

A year or two after my initiation into the ranks of the vaqueros, I was working for Fred Fickert with Francisco Martinez. One day, old Martinez and I rode to the Tehachapi Cattle Company's Bear Mountain Ranch nearby. As we passed through a gate on nearing the ranch we saw a man saddling a horse, and before we reached him, he had mounted and was riding to meet us. He rode up and said, "*¿Que hay, Martinez?*" (How goes it, Martinez), in that manner of speech found only in California, and which is so delightful to hear that it makes one glad to have been born to the Spanish language.

"*Hay que tenemos hambre, Encinas* (How it goes is that we are hungry, Encinas)," replied Martinez. Encinas! So this was the vaquero whom I had admired because of the brown horse. I stared at him. He was a man in early middle age, but he was already, like Martinez, bowed and stooped. His hands were rope gnarled and his face was weather beaten. A man of tough racial constitution, the product of a combination of races, the blood of conquistadores and Indians in his veins. Here, I thought, was a man who probably saw no glory in herding cattle, but took it with all its dangers, its discomforts, its risks and hardships without complaint; stoical, yet with a sense of humor that made even danger and thirst amusing. A survivor of survivors, of slaughtered Moors and Indians. The result of generations of men inured to the saddle and molded ever seen him was never to change in all the years I knew him, not even after he had come to live with me in his old age. by hard riding and short commons into the toughness of whang leather.

This was the man whom I had come to know through a brown horse, and the estimate I had made of him before I had

"*Vengan a comer, pues* (Come and eat, then)," he invited us.

It wasn't that we were actually hungry, so much as that we were tired of the gringo food which we got at Fickert's, and wanted something that would stick to our ribs, such as frijoles, tortillas and roasted beef ribs.

After his wife had given us food and we had eaten well, the three of us mounted up and rode away over a hill into a little flat where there were some calves. We came to a tree from which hung a gunny sack. Adolfo dismounted and took down the sack from the tree and emptied its contents on the ground: a sixty foot service-worn reata and a pair of Garcia spurs. The vaquero strapped the reata to the saddle and the spurs to his heels and mounted his horse. We rode off toward the calves.

Suddenly Martinez pointed to a calf and said, "*Mira hay esta un hinchado* (Look, there is one that is swollen)."

"*¡Y hay otro, y otro!* (And there is another, and another,

and another)." Adolfo took down his reata and made a loop, and pointing at a calf, said to me, "*Hecha ese pa' 'ca* (Drive that one toward me)."

I drove a calf toward him, and as it came within range of his reata, he threw a *lazo* around its neck. Martinez then threw his loop around its hind legs.

I tailed it down and held it while Adolfo dismounted and doctored it for the screw-worms with which it was infected.

When we had treated all the calves, we rode back to the tree where Adolfo unstrapped his reata from the saddle and the spurs from his heels, put them in the sack, and hung it back in the tree again. We then rode back to the Bear Mountain Ranch where we left Adolfo, and from there we continued our journey to Fickert's.

On the way I asked Martinez why Adolfo kept his reata and spurs hung in a tree away from the ranch. Martinez told me that because Roland Hill, the manager of the Tehachapi Cattle Company, bred the finest Morgans in North America, the vaqueros were strictly forbidden to wear spurs or to carry reatas. Roland didn't want to take a chance of his horses getting hurt or spoiled.

"Well," I said, "why doesn't Adolfo let the calves go to hell until the boss sees them, instead of roping them against orders."

"If he waited until Roland happened to see the calves most of them would be dead," Martinez said, "and Adolfo is too good a man to let that happen."

Here was a man who took such pride in his calling that he disobeyed the boss's orders to save the boss's property! No wonder the brown had been such a good horse; he couldn't have been anything else with such a man for a master.

Chapter 6

HORSES AND HORSEMEN

When an experienced horseman went to work on a ranch, he was prepared to meet any kind of a horse, for all ranches had horses with bad habits. However, bucking was not considered a bad habit, because many otherwise faultless vaquero horses were buckers. Being thrown off a horse was a big incentive to a rider to stay aboard next time. Land Company horses carried the blood of Salvator and other fountainheads of the thoroughbred breed in America, horses that had been famous on the turf. After the Haggin breeding farm, Rancho Del Paso was closed, the remaining horses were shipped to Stockdale, the company horse breeding ranch. The buckaroos there, as a result, were mounted on some of the finest horse flesh in the country. When a Land Company horse moved, he moved fast.

In the course of his peregrinations from one ranch to another, sooner or later the buckaroo encountered all manner of horses—runaways, buckers, cinchbinders. But the barnstale or barnsour horse was unknown on the ranches. A barnstale horse is an animal that has been kept in his stall so long that he refuses to leave it. He will balk when he has been ridden a short distance. He will then rear and try to run back to the barn. The vaquero horses did not acquire this habit because of the practice on the ranches of turning the horses out to pasture after they had been ridden. In fact, many horses were ridden after cattle all their lives without ever seeing the inside of a barn.

Horses were thrown, saddled, mounted and ridden the first time they made their acquaintance with men, so naturally they bucked. Hunger makes good bull fighters, and by the same token, necessity makes good riders. Having to ride rough horses over rough country makes for balance, and there is no royal road to acquiring it, since muscle has to be developed before one has balance, and the only way muscle can be acquired is by long hours in the saddle.

One rider has a firm seat, but a poor bridle hand; another rider cannot be bucked off, but he cannot guide a horse correctly; and yet another may have a good bridle hand, but a poor seat. Only the rider with a sensitive hand has good horses.

In horse training, years alone do not suffice. Many men never qualify as horse trainers because they do not have an affinity with the horses, though they may ride horses for years.

Ranch horses were bred from different light horse breeds. Most of them were descended from the original Spanish horse. A good horse, no matter what breed, was an individual. A good vaquero horse, was, first of all, intelligent, and breeding had nothing to do with it. The practice of letting horses run on the open range through their colthood was conducive to their learning to take care of themselves; and the practice of not breaking them until after they were past four-and-a-half years old was another factor in developing good horses. Once broken and in the saddle horse band (*caponera*), they were seldom, if ever, confined in a stall. And excepting the short time they were held in a corral to be caught, they were not restrained. They were driven from one camp to another, and thus stayed in hard condition and able to do a day's work at all times.

Horses that had Spanish blood showed it in their dun or slate color with a line down their back. The Appaloosa, however, was never common in California.

The horses that more nearly approached their Andalusian "Barb" ancestors had sloping shoulders, rounded quarters (called "coyote" hips) and the ram heads with tiny pin ears.

They were smaller than the other horses, but few of the larger horses had the courage of the mustangs. The Spanish horse was bred out by crossing with the wrong horse. And it was not until toward the end of the ranching era that horses were bred into good saddle stock again by breeding to light horse stallions. It is to be regretted that the original horse was not selected and bred up as he has been in Spain and Argentina. He had already become perfectly adapted to climatic and working conditions.

The vaquero relied on his horse, and the horse relied on his rider. If the vaquero had sense enough to let the horse use his intelligence there would be a perfect harmony between horse and rider. True, horses were often overworked, but that was not the fault of the vaquero. It was a condition of all cattle countries. The vaquero was naturally kind, and although he was never known to pet his horse, he never forgot to feed it.

Men who were rough on horses soon got a reputation on all the ranches and were accordingly despised. Such a man was never called cruel, he was called *hereje* (heretic). This came to us from the time of the Moors in Spain, when Christians attributed everything vile to those of another faith, even as we do this day.

A good foreman would try to get the work done by having the rider ride well. He would try to fit the man to the horse by mounting the vaquero on a horse that had a like disposition. In working cattle the horse accepts his rider as his partner and works the beef as his enemy. A rider who had aptitude for teaching a horse could keep the animal behind a cow and let the horse teach himself.

Horses would sometimes acquire the habit of falling over backwards after being cinched-up. And it was seldom that a vaquero escaped injury when a horse threw himself over backwards with the rider in the saddle. A blue mare on the Deep Wells Ranch at Buttonwillow fell over backwards with a young fellow named Bert Tibbets. Tibbets' spleen burst.

Johnnie Drayer on San Emideo suffered a broken leg when

a gray fell over. He was on crutches for many months afterwards. It is one of the worst experiences a man can meet.

Another chilling experience is to have a horse stampede, or run away. However, this seldom happened. The only horse that would stampede, that this writer remembers, was a dunnish bay called "El Diablo" on San Emideo Ranch. He came from one of the other Land Company ranches, where he had been spoiled. On his arrival at San Emideo the foreman Ramon Feliz saddled him and rode him off. The horse stampeded over a cliff and fell in a ravine. When Ramon failed to show up the men went out to look for him. They found him lying hurt at the bottom of the ravine. Later George Brunk took Diablo and got work out of him; but he was the only one who ever did. For some reason the horse never attempted to run away with him.

The San Joaquin had once been an immense swamp, and in wet winters some parts of the valley would become flooded, compelling the vaqueros to cross water. This led to much merriment because some amusing incident never failed to occur. There was tragedy, too, sometimes. Pedro Carmelo was riding across a slough when his horse stepped into a ravine hidden under water and fell. Pedro fell under the horse, and the animal in his struggle stepped on him and he was drowned.

The rider who is afraid of water and pulls his feet up loses control of his horse. The rider in water must look up, never down. Men who are riding in water are inclined to look down at the eddies and whirlpools, which causes a turning sensation and throws the rider off balance. The rider must act so that when the water's depth and pressure increases, and he and his horse have to swim, neither one will lose his head.

Crossing cattle over water with a current is not an easy task. A beef unfamiliar with water will try to place his feet on something on which to gain a foothold and climb. As often as not, it will place its feet on the animal in front of it. When the current of a canal or river presses against a herd of cattle, the cattle form a dam above which the water is checked. The depth increases and causes an increasing pressure which pushes the animal downstream.

The range rider soon learned that the hardest way to decide the length of stirrups he should use was by losing them when riding a bucking horse. Over a period of time he learned that too long a stirrup would be lost, and when they were lost he would lose his balance and his seat. Short stirrups indicate a balanced rider. Long stirrups indicate that the rider depends on grip. The more expert older vaqueros, in their overweening pride, rode long stirrups.

No tenia mano (he had no hand) was a term that described an unfortunate with horses, a man who had no luck with them. If he started to break a horse the horse would turn out a bucker. If he finished breaking it, the horse would be hard-mouthed. If he fed animals, they would not thrive; if he altered a calf, the calf would die; or if he branded one, the brand would be smudged.

CHAPTER 7

THERE ARE TRICKS IN ALL TRADES

The sorrel colt had been ridden too long in the *jaquima* and, as a result, had become habituated to it. The rancher had tried every bit he owned on the horse, but he would work in none. Then the rancher, who had spent time going to school when he should have been riding and studying horses, gave up hope of ever bitting the horse. He was ready to turn him out until such time as a buyer should come along, when one morning a white-haired old man on a fleabitten gray mare rode up to the ranchhouse gate and stopped to study the barns and corrals and the animals in them. The appearance of the buildings and the condition of the livestock told the old man all he needed to know of the rancher's character, and he knew what sort of person he had to deal with. He dismounted, tied the old gray to the fence and stepped through the gate. He walked up to the rancher and asked, "Do you have any horses here that have bad teeth and won't bit up or fatten up? I float horses' teeth." The rancher looked into the old man's face and liked what he saw. And just as the old man had judged the rancher by the condition of his ranch and livestock, so had the rancher judged the old man by the cut of his lean old face and that air of a horse master about him. So he said, "I have a horse here that I am about ready to sell for chicken feed. I rode him two years in the *jaquima*. He will not work on a bit and turns his head sidewise when I exert a pull on the reins. My father was taught to ride by the old-time California spade bit men. He was one of the best reinsmen in the country and left me a number of good bits, but none seem to work on this horse."

"Do you mind if I take a look at your horse?" the old man asked.

The rancher led him to a corral where a rangy, clean-limbed sorrel gelding was munching hay. The old man stepped into the corral and walked slowly around the gelding, taking in his fine, lean, long neck and deep barrel. He ran his hand over the horse's back muscles, then grasped the tail and pulled to see if the horse would resist. A good horse will always resist the pull, even if he is ready to drop from exhaustion, and this sorrel did not disappoint the old man. With a satisfied smile he turned to the rancher.

"This is too good a horse to sell for chicken feed. Let's see what we can do for him."

He walked to his horse and untied a bundle from the saddle, and took it back to the sorrel. He tied a rope around the horse's neck and backed him into a corner. Then he reached into the animal's mouth, grasped the tongue and pulled it out. Holding it firmly so the horse couldn't bite, he ran a finger along the edges of the upper molars. They were sharp as knives.

"Do you see these hooks?" he asked the rancher. "They are cutting into the cheeks and are causing the horse to turn his head when you pull on the reins."

He reached into the sack and brought out a float. He then proceeded to rasp the edges of the horse's teeth. He rasped until the sound and feel of the tool told him that the teeth were smooth. He took the float out of the horse's mouth and showed the rancher what he had done to the teeth.

"The upper jaw is wider than the lower," he explained, "and over a period of time the upper teeth wear at an angle and develop sharp edges. I rasped the edges off. Now, let's take a look at your bits."

The old man found good equipment in the saddle room. Some of the bits had been made by Tapia, some by Manuel

Gil, and others by Miguel Morales. He examined each bit, one by one, and at last selected the Tapia with the highest spade. He carried it to the watering trough and immersed it in the water. Then he asked the rancher for some salt. When it was brought he sprinkled it over the mouthpiece, attached a headstall to the bit and hung it back on the wall.

"The salt will cake," he said, "and tomorrow we will go to work on the sorrel. He can be bitted, but it will take a long time and a lot of patience to do the job. Be sure you don't feed him tonight. He's too fat anyhow, and going without feed for one night won't hurt. I'll be back tomorrow."

The next morning the old man arrived at sunup. He unsaddled the gray and turned him into a corral. Then he untied two rubber strips, about four feet long and about two inches wide, which he had brought tied to the saddle. The rancher watched every move the old man made. The old man caught the horse and saddled him. Then he bridled him with the bit he had sprinkled with salt the day before. He fastened the rubber strips to the bit as he would have fitted a pair of reins, pulling the slack out of them and tying them to the horn. Then he turned the sorrel loose in the corral. He went to the haystack, picked up a forkful of hay and took it to the corral where he scattered it in little piles along the fence. Then he walked out and closed the gate behind him.

The sorrel had not eaten all night. He approached the hay and bent his head to get a mouthful. The rubber reins stretched until he had almost reached the hay, when suddenly the stretch went out of the rubber and the pull became strong enough to make him lift his head. He backed a step, then tried again to reach the hay, but again had to lift his head before he reached the hay. The old man chuckled.

"He will keep trying and will in time bit himself up," he explained. "The pull on the rubber is slight until he almost reaches the hay, then the pull becomes strong enough to make him lift his head. The high port prevents him from laying on the bit and lugging as he would if it were a bit with a low port.

The high port also keeps him from getting his tongue over the mouthpiece. The high port will hit the roof of his mouth and make him pull his chin in toward his chest so that it may rest on his tongue. Now, if you will saddle and bit him up as I have done every morning until I come back, I think he will take the bit. It would be best to feed him only in the evening from now on, never in the morning. But be sure you don't ride him until I get back."

"How long will you be gone?" the rancher asked.

"Oh, about a couple of weeks," the old man replied.

But it was a full month before the old man rode the gray horse up to the ranchhouse gate again. The rancher had been bitting the horse every morning and leaving him bitted all day. One look told the old man that the horse had made a habit of the bit and was ready to go to work. The old man went into the saddle room and picked up a pair of rawhide reins, and returned to the corral where the sorrel was contentedly spinning the cricket in the bit. He removed the rubber strips from the bit and attached the rawhide reins, then led the sorrel out to the rancher.

"Here, get on your horse and see if he will work now."

The rancher mounted and rode the horse out to a field where a number of steers were grazing. He rode into the herd and parted out a steer, then a second, then a third; the sorrel neither threw his head nor turned it sidewise. He kept his chin tucked in and his ears cocked forward. Satisfied, the rancher rode back to where the old man was waiting.

"He worked perfectly!" the rancher exclaimed.

The old man said dryly, "Well, there are more ways to kill a cat than by choking it in milk."

After the rancher had paid him generously, and the old man was riding away through the gate, he turned in his saddle and called out, "Remember, for every day you keep a bit out of a horse's mouth, you lose part of his rein."

Chapter 8

STORIES AND SKETCHES

A STRIKE FOR HIGHER WAGES

Don Jesus Lopez was manager or *mayordomo* and Don Porfirio Valencia was the *caporal*; Chico Martinez, Antonio Araujo, Pablo Apodaca, Bob Addington, Nepomuseno Cordero, Willie Husband, Juan Bravo and I (Adolfo Encinas) were in the crew gathering cattle on the Tejon Ranch, when Turner Rose and George Brunk, San Emido Ranch buckaroos, were sent to the Tejon to "rep" (represent) the Kern County Land Company during the rodeos. They were old friends of some of the members of the Tejon crew, having worked with them at one time or another on one of the many ranches in the great valley. Since both were very good buckaroos and genial, likable men, they were soon very much at home with the entire crew. In the evenings, in the talks around the campfire, the two buckaroos learned that the Tejon vaqueros were paid only forty dollars a month, while the Land Company riders were paid forty-five. Turner and George advised the Tejon men to go on strike for higher wages. Turner, who was something of a bunkhouse lawyer, urged, "Now is the time; the boss needs men, and he will pay."

Accordingly, the elected spokesman of the vaqueros, with some hesitation, approached the respected old *mayordomo*, Don Jesus Lopez, and said, "Don Jesus *cuarenta pesos son muy pocos. Nosotros queremos que usted nos suba los sueldos* (Don Jesus, forty dollars is too little, we want you to raise our wages)."

Adolfo, who told the story, here chuckled reminiscently and fondly, saying, "*¡Caramba! se le paro el poco pelo que tenia a Don Jesus* (The few hairs that remained to Don Jesus stood up on end)." Never in the long history of the Tejon Ranch had a demand for higher wages been heard.

Don Jesus stammered, "*¡Vamos al rancho, todos, y lleven todo el ganado, vamos!* (Go to the ranch, everyone, and take all the cattle, go!)"

When the vaqueros got to the ranch Don Jesus snapped, "*¡Amarren sus caballos, y vengas a la oficina!* (Tie your horses and come to the office!)"

Don Porfirio, the *caporal*, was in the office when Don Jesus called in the men one by one. When they were all assembled he turned to the *caporal* and said "*Esto, Porfirio, no es mas culpa de esos cabrones vaqueros gringoes* (This, Porfirio, is no fault of anyone but of those billygoat gringo vaqueros)."

"*Thi thenor Don Jethus,*" Don Porfirio lisped, "*no puede thar math que de elloth* (Yes sir Don Jesus, it could not be of any other than of theirs)."

Don Jesus then turned to the vaqueros' spokesman and expostulated, "*¡Mas sueldo, sus sueldos son muy altos ya!* (More wages! Your wages are very high already!)"

"*Los vaqueros de la Compania guanan cuarenta-y-cinco pesos* (The Company vaqueros are paid forty-five dollars)," the spokesman argued doggedly.

"*¿Quien te dijo ese?* (Who told you that?)"

"*Los vaquero de San Emido.* (The vaqueros from San Emido)."

"*¡Que cabrones son esos vaqueros!* (What billygoats those vaqueros are!)"

"*Pero tengo muy poco trabajo para ustedes* (But I have very little work for you)."

"*Usted tiene toda la Sierra y el disierto* (distant section of the ranch) *para trabajar. Los rodeos nomás están comensando.* (You have all the Sierra and the desert to work. The rodeos are just commencing.)"

Don Jesus studied the matter for a few moments and said, "*Bueno, por una temporadita, pero por una temporadita nomas, les voy a subir los sueldos* (For a little while, but for only a little while, no more, I am going to raise your wages)."

But Don Jesus never lowered the wages, as he had hinted; he kept on paying forty-five dollars a month.

One morning, after the rodeos were over and all the extra men had been laid off, we were in the corral catching our horses when the old Don walked in and said, "*Muchachos, quiero que agarren potrillos, vamos a sacar todos los caballitos viejos de la caponero y soltarlos para que descansen, y vamos a ensillar potrillos. Les voy a pagar cinco pesos mas por cada potrillo que amansen.* (Boys, I want you to catch up the colts. We shall take all the old horses out of the saddle-horse band, and turn them out so that they may rest, and we shall ride colts. I am going to pay you five dollars extra for every horse that you break.)"

All of us—I, Lupe Gomez, Willie Husband, Antonio Araujo and even Juan Gomez, who had only one leg—took a horse to break.

Oddly enough, Don Jesus never held a grudge against George Brunk for being the instigator of the strike for higher wages. Whenever the vaqueros were camped at the Lecheria near Lebec, Don Jesus would order the cook to cut some choice pieces of meat and to make a present of them to "the gringo billygoat" who lived near the camp of the vaqueros.

THE QUEST

For some years now I have been collecting old saddlery catalogs, old saddles, spurs, bits and other articles which are getting scarce as the years roll by. I revel in the possession of these things and trust that some day I shall have a place to put them where I can spend time in their contemplation. They will bring memories of the old days on the ranches, of Juan Olivera, Luis Zamora, Juan Gomez, Bill Nickles, Dick Kelly, George Brunk, George Hoskings, Catarino Reese, Clarence Clark and others who rode the range.

Old center-fire saddles are becoming hard to find, and when one is found it behooves the finder to buy it, if he can persuade the owner to part with it, and once in possession of it, to give thanks for having found a treasure.

One day I came upon one at an auction and bought it. I took it home to feast my eyes upon it and to dream back to the days when these old saddles were used, and of the men who used them, a half century ago.

But my joy was short lived. On examining my treasure I found that it was not complete. The saddle lacked a cinch, the thirty-two strand mane-hair cinch with the diamond design worked into the center and the tassel which hangs down, as one invariably sees in Russell pictures. My quest was by no means finished. I must yet find the cinch to complete the saddle, for no self-respecting old timer would have ridden a saddle without a mane-hair cinch.

I went from saddlery to saddlery, from second hand store to second hand store, from antique shop to antique shop without success; mane-hair cinches were not to be found. Weary and hopeless I came at last to Jedlicka's Saddlery in Santa Barbara. There, in his back room was an old Garcia saddle with a thirty-two strand mane-hair cinch.

I said, "I will pay you the price of a new cinch for this old cinch."

"No, we must sell this saddle with the cinch."

"But," I argued, "I already have a saddle, all I need is the cinch."

The final answer was, "No," so I bought the saddle to get the cinch.

When I arrived in Bakersfield I showed my treasure to an old timer and told him the story. He looked the cinch over carefully and said, "This cinch has been used on a pot-bellied horse. The action of the horse's forequarters have broken the first three strands. The horse was a bucker, or the cinch's former owner was a rider of bucking horses; because the leather guards on the cinch rings are pitted with holes made by the rowells of the rider's spurs when he used the spurs to stay on by hooking them into the cinch. He was a California man, even if he used a Nevada saddle, because he used spurs with very small rowells. The holes made by the rowells are set very close together."

So I not only acquired a "find" for my collection, but its history as well.

APPALOOSA

The common belief current among Appaloosa breeders and enthusiasts is that the Appaloosa was ridden into Europe by the Tartars from central Asia when the mongol hordes overran most of Europe and that the horse was scattered when the Huns were defeated at Chalons. His hogged mane and sparsely haired tail indicate a Tarpan-like ancestor, and his appearance agrees with the Spaniards' contention that the Andalusian originated in the Tarpan-like horse of Spain.

My study of and admiration for the Appaloosa horse began fifty years ago when I was riding on the southern division of Miller and Lux Ranches. The Southern Division spread over several counties. I was helping to gather cattle on the Carrisso Plains in San Luis Obispo County.

We were driving a bunch of cattle toward the rodeo grounds at Painted Rock Pump when a band of spotted horses raced past us on their way to water. We stopped to study them as they crowded around the trough at Painted Rock Springs. While there were a few solid colored animals in the band, most of them were of the leopard or blanket color pattern. Their odd coloring prompted one of the riders to exclaim, "Oh, look at the Arabian horses!"

But another member of our crew who had a deeper knowledge of horses, scoffed, "Arabians, hell, those are Appaloosas."

We were to learn that the animals we were discussing had come originally from the wild range bands captured by Indian horse hunters and brought into Elko, Nevada, for shipment to market. G. S. Garcia, a resident of Elko, selected the best horses from each band brought in. When he had gathered a carload he would ship them to his brother at the Saucito Ranch on the Carrisso Plains.

Mr. Garcia had an eye for a good horse. All the Appaloosas in the band were good, big, rangy animals.

Since that time I have had the opportunity to study other horses of the breed. In 1927 or '28 I was riding for Paul Michel at his stable near Griffith Park in Los Angeles County. At a neighboring stable there were thirty Appaloosa geldings that had been shipped from Argentina. They were all very good examples of horse flesh, mostly of the leopard color pattern. The Argentines in charge of them called them *criollos* (creoles). They told me that the horses descended from animals left on the Pampas by the viceroy Pedro De Mendoza. The horses were being broken in at the time and quite often I had a chance to see them "break in two" with their rider. Those *criollos* could buck high, wide and handsome.

In the late 1940's I found little Appaloosas in the states of Jalisco and Colima in Central Mexico. Though they did not weigh more than six hundred pounds, they were as tough as rawhide. The Mexicans told me that their little Appaloosas, which they call *"Guinduris"* (the *guinduri* is a spotted cat) were descended from the royal Austrian horses (probably Lippizans) brought into Mexico by the invading French troops under Maximillian, Archduke of Austria.

Throughout a half century of studying the breed—if it can be called a breed—I have been struck with the similarity in horses that come from widely separated parts of the New World. All the horses, those from the state of Nevada, from Argentina and central Mexico, had the same color patterns—the wall eye, the sparsely haired mane and tail. Even their conformation was similar, at least in the shape of their hips and set of their tail.

While studying horses in Europe I learned that all European Appaloosas had a Spanish background and that there have been Appaloosa-colored horses in Spain since stone-age men hunted horses for food and learned to depict their successes in the chase by making crude drawings on the walls of their caves. Old illustrations of horses of the Spanish Riding School (Lippizans) often are depicted in the Appaloosa color patterns.

The leopard horse of Denmark, the Knabstrup, descends from a Spanish mare taken to that country by a captain of cavalry. The Austrian Kladruber and Pinzgauer, often of Appaloosa coloring, have Spanish blood. While they can hardly be called a "light horse" they were at one time used for cavalry mounts, as were all present day draft horse breeds.

SPANISH CATTLE

Don Gaspar De Portola brought the first herd of Spanish cattle for the missions into California in 1769, and Don Juan Bautiste De Anza brought the second (this was the first herd of settlers' cattle) in 1776.

Ewing Young, the trapper, drove the first herd of cattle out of California into Oregon in 1836. This was the first of what might be called a "trail herd" in the history of the West. Young may very well be called the father of the trail driving industry, for he set a pattern which was to be followed over all the continent.

Other cattle drovers soon began to follow his example and after 1846 began moving great herds of cattle and horses to the East and North.

Young had made a contract with the settlers of the Willamette Valley in Oregon to supply them with stock cattle. At the start of his drive he met with many difficulties and was stalled several times. He finally hired a crew of vaqueros to drive his animals.

Those cattle were all of the Spanish breed. It was not until 1840 that well bred cattle were brought over the Oregon Trail to improve the Spanish breed. It was not long before Red Durhams began to show their influence on the cattle of the western ranges. Henry Miller bought a herd of red cattle from Hildreth Brothers soon after he had established himself in the meat business in San Francisco. That was the first time he saw the double H, the brand he was to put on many thousands of head of cattle roaming on millions of acres of land.

There were millions of head of cattle in California when the gringos came in 1846. The statement that cattle were brought to California from Texas is absurd; there were more cattle here than there were in Texas despite the fact that the migration of gold seekers put an end to the raising of cattle for hides and created a market for beef, and despite the fact that thousands of head had been driven out of this state over the Spanish and Mormon Trails. During the heavy floods of 1862 many herds were drowned, and the droughts that followed on the heels of the floods were responsible for the loss of a million head of cattle in southern California alone.

It is hard to comprehend, under the circumstances, why anyone would try to bring cattle from the Gulf Coast when this state was swarming with cattle which could be had for the taking. There were so many wild cattle in the San Joaquin Valley that Charlie Kerr kept a crew of men roping and branding ownerless cattle. There is a story to the effect that Charlie let his vaqueros keep part of the cattle that they caught in payment for their work! Of course this is not true—it was often said around the campfire, especially when the vaqueros had had a grueling day, that all a vaquero or buckaroo needed to qualify for his work was a strong back and weak mind—but even a vaquero or buckaroo couldn't have been that stupid. Nevertheless, Charlie accumulated a large herd of cattle during his lifetime.

Furthermore, it was said that the country between here and Texas was full of cattle, that the Mormon Battalion on its way to California found thousands of cattle on its route and the troops had to force their way through the herds. It was also reported that bulls attacked the troopers. It is doubtful if any cattle came from Texas to the actual West. If there had been any cattle from the Gulf Coast in Montana in the 1880's Charles M. Russell would have seen them, for he was a very observant man. But Russell's riders were Oregon buckaroos, the riggings of his riders' saddles were centerfire, the bits were Spanish spades, the cattle were half-bred Oregon Durhams and the horses were big-boned Oregon mustangs. The cowboy of the period used a Frazier double rig saddle and a grazer bit, his cattle were supposed to be longhorns, and his horses were ponies.

WISDOM

"A man never starts to learn until he discovers that he knows nothing," is one of the most quoted of the many old sayings heard on the ranches.

The young ranch manager was as green as grass. His only qualification for the job was that he had been to school and could read and write. He had inherited a good vaquero boss from the previous manager, and like a smart captain who has a good sergeant, he knew the man's value. But the vaquero boss had gone on a cattle drive and the manager was facing a problem which he would have to solve alone.

Henry Miller had arrived with a herd of cattle for the ranch, and the manager did not know what price to offer for them. He went to Miller and said, "Mr. Miller, I don't know what to offer for the cattle. I am going to let you set the price. I know that you would never take advantage of me."

Even an old time horse trader would not have taken advantage of a man who exhibited so much trust and frankness.

Miller not only did not take advantage, he quoted a price below the current market level, so that when the vaquero boss returned he was surprised at the old cattle king's generosity.

But Miller was not always so inclined to magnanimity. A cattleman who prided himself on his ability to judge beef offered to sell Miller a herd of one thousand head at ten cents a pound. Miller offered seven cents a pound. The cattleman refused.

Miller then said, "I will give you ten cents for my pick of five hundred, and five cents for the rest." The cattleman agreed.

Miller parted out five hundred of the smallest and thinnest of the steers and paid the cattleman ten cents, then paid five cents for the rest. When the accounts were settled it was found that he had bought the cattle for less than the seven cents he had offered.

Years later when the same manager had grown wise and experienced, he told me that Miller had taught him how to estimate a herd. His technique was to part out ten head from one side of a herd, then estimate each beef's weight, add the ten weights and strike an average; then go to the other side of the herd and part out ten, estimate, add, and average their weight as he did the first ten, then add up the two average weights.

The result, divided by two should yield the average for the herd.

FIESTA

It is the 4th of October and the *Fiesta De San Francisco* is in full swing in Magdalena, Sonora, Mexico. A stream of *penitentes* crowds into the maze of ramshackle booths set up in the two plazas of the town. These people have walked into the old Kino mission town from all directions, some from as far as the border sixty miles away; and though the clergy of late frowns on the practice, the devout continue the pilgrimages. Ambulances are kept busy day and night bringing in the pilgrims who, exhausted, fall by the wayside.

The people hold the image of San Francisco, which is kept in the church, in great reverence, whatever their beliefs may be, for it helps the town. The influx of people during the *fiesta* brings in money which could never be earned in any other way in this desert cowtown. Without the image, life in Magdalena would be hard indeed.

In front of the church a Yaqui dances a *pascola* (an Indian dance). The wail of the flute and the beat of the tom-tom bring odd stirrings to a man of mixed blood. The maggots of bitterness and resentment begin to eat at one's brain. They bring an urge to rise and fight against tyranny and oppression, to pit naked breast against steel-tipped lance, and to die in defiance, a feeling that death would be well met selling one's life dearly.

The Yaqui dancer sweats profusely, and an elderly *señora* steps out of the crowd. She draws a fine handkerchief out of a purse and wipes the Indian's brown back. She lays a few coppers on the ground and walks away. No one seems surprised at her action. It is an act of humility. It is, in effect, the ages-old rite of washing the beggar's feet.

The beat of the tom-tom dies away, the wail of the flute fades. The dancer removes his deerhead headdress, picks up the coppers on the ground, and walks away. One is suddenly aware of the music coming from a doorway. It is an Andalusian song. One listens to the Moorish wail and dreams of homeric *conquistadores* marching over half a world and taking it for their own, hare-brained men who succeeded from sheer audacity; and for a moment one is proud.

An odd heritage, this mixture of Yaqui, Mayo, Moor, Goth, Jew and Basque blood.

PORTRAIT OF A PIONEER

It was the annual Tracy Ranch barbecue with its atmosphere of old-time hospitality, so typical of the pioneer family.

We sat in the shade of the towering eucalyptus trees that surround the house, and Mrs. Tracy, eighty years old, said, "There were no trees on the west side of the valley when we came here. We had to plant these."

Her trees are now landmarks and can be seen from miles away.

"One of our chief pastimes when we were children was spearing lizards," she reminisced.

"What did you do with them after you had speared them?" she was asked.

"Nothing, our only object was to see how many we could spear.

"We rode all the calves on the ranch too. I made a good saddle animal out of a little steer. He was as good as a horse, and easy riding."

From Mrs. Tracy's conversation one can understand why her sons, some thirty years ago, gained a reputation for doing stunts which put them in danger of breaking their necks: little pastimes such as riding bucking horses and Brahma bulls backwards.

After the barbecue, which was excellent, we went out to the corrals to see the youngest generation of Tracys put on a rodeo.

A number of husky calves were in a chute for the kids to ride. A tow-headed grandson would be put aboard one of the calves, and turned into the arena. Each of the tykes, it is needless to say, rode his calf.

One calf bucked across the arena and fell with his rider. For a while the boy lay quite still. His mother and several friends went out to help him, but he got up and walked away. I am sure I detected a trace of swagger in his walk.

I came away that evening secure in the thought that the

younger Tracys had not lost any of the spirit which had made their grandparents pioneers.

RANCH HORSES

Ranch horses survive in spite of man's inhumane treatment of them. Sometimes I wake at night and think back to the days on the ranches and wonder if I'll go to hell for what I did with horses. We would often ride a horse to the end of his endurance through a twelve hour day, and come in on a freezing night, take the saddle off, and turn him out wet with sweat to scrounge what he could in an alfalfa field that had been frozen down to the roots. How they survived, I don't know. They must have kept moving instinctively to keep warm and to dry their coats.

Before daylight one morning Max Gomez, the Spanish Basque and I left Pimentel Ranch on the Carriso Plains, and all through that morning we stood up in our stirrups and rode as we put mile after mile behind us. His horse paced and mine trotted side by side with each one's nose stretched eagerly forward.

Max rode a chunky, apple rumped little Nevada mustang who, no doubt, had inherited his pacing gait from some distant Spanish palfrey. I rode a big leggy bay of coach blood that travelled with that clean, springy, mile devouring trot for which horses of that breed are famous the world over.

At noon we came to a lonely sheep camp out on the sunburnt plain where we stopped for an hour. The Basque herder, glad for our company, gave us a meal of browned lamb chops, friend potatoes, sour dough bread, which only the Basques know how to bake, and a glass of his hoarded red wine.

When our horses had finished the grain we had brought for them, we mounted and through that long afternoon and evening we stood up in our stirrups again and rode; and through that long afternoon and evening our horses never faltered. They were still travelling side by side with their noses stretched eagerly forward when at nine o'clock that night we rode into Klipstein's ranch in Santa Barbara Canyon. We had covered eighty miles in sixteen hours.

The next morning we held a rodeo and gathered the Miller and Lux cattle that had been running with Klipstein's cattle. That evening we made it back as far as the Whim Ranch of the Kern County Land Company and on the third day we were back at Pimentel Ranch.

SERIS

Of all the Indians who haunted the deserts touching the banks of the Colorado—Seri, Apache, Yaqui—the Seri was the most feared. Yet he did not compare as a warrior with the other tribesmen. The reason for the fear was that the Seri was said to eat the flesh of his victims. Even today the belief that the Seri is a cannibal is common throughout the desert country. Children are still frightened by being told that they will be eaten if they are disobedient. Whether the charge of cannibalism has any basis in fact, we do not know. It is most probably just another of the many slanders that have been brought against Indians since the white man began to covet their property three centuries ago. In any case, whatever the Seri may have been in the past, he is now harmless, and only a few of the tribesmen survive.

Actually the Seri is one of the finest physical specimens found among aborigines. His powers of endurance are unbelievable. He can outrun a horse and often runs down his game. He likes his meat gamey, and whenever he kills or comes upon a freshly killed animal, he does not immediately dress it, but sets up a pole to guide him back to it, then goes away and leaves it. After a few days, when the carcass is "ripe" he returns and prepares it for eating.

The Seri is very fond of horseflesh and seems to prefer it to other meat.

We had rounded up a band of horses for a rancher south of the *Gran Desierto* along the shores of the Gulf of California. In the band were a number of cripples and old useless animals which the ranchers cull out and discard. The Seris had gathered at the corral on the off-chance that the rancher would let them have the discards of the band for food.

When the horses had been driven into the corrals and the ranchero had looked them over, he called to the Seri chief and said, pointing to an old mare and colt, "I will give you that mare and colt if you will bring me a deer."

The Seri turned and without a word trotted off. Late that afternoon he appeared driving a little buck deer before him. The Indian carried a long switch cut from a mesquite and whenever he wished to turn the little buck he would hit it on the horns with the switch. The deer would turn away from the blow. The deer was staggering from exhaustion, but the Seri did not appear tired.

We parted out the old mare and drove her through the corral gate. She ran off toward the open range, and when she had covered about a hundred yards, the rancher gave a signal. Four of the Indians leaped after her, and before she had covered another hundred yards, the Seris had overtaken her. They leaped upon her and bore her to the ground. In a few minutes they had slit her throat and cut her up in quarters and were drinking the fluid from her belly. They went through the same performance with the colt.

The people of that desert country believe that the Seris are *hechiseros* (practitioners of witchcraft). One of the vaqueros told me of once having had an experience with Seri witchcraft. He and the Seri had gathered a small band of wild horses and driven them to the gates of a corral. But the horses would not pass through the gate. They had almost run their horses down trying to get the broncos into the corral when the Seri dismounted and walked to a corner of the corral.

From there he walked in a straight line a few paces and set his shirt down. Here he turned and walked a few paces and set his blanket down. He had paced and marked off an imaginary corral wing. Then he got on his horse and we drove the mustangs toward the gate again. But to my great surprise they would not cross over the imaginary wing the Seri had made with the articles of clothing. After a break or two back we drove them through the gate and closed it.

CANTLEBERRY

Bill Cantleberry learned to ride when the word vaquero was not synonymous with cowboy. To Bill, a man who herded cattle for a living was not a "cowhand" nor a "cowpoke" nor yet a "cowboy"; he was a vaquero. And Bill was a "bukera" as he pronounced it.

"If you don't learn to ride before you are twenty," he said, "it is too late and you never learn. I ran away from home when I was thirteen years old on a little pony my father had paid six bits for."

"The first job I had was on the Cox and Clark Ranch. In those days a horse that had been lassed (lassoed) and thrown was considered a broke horse and one that did not fall over backwards was considered a gentle horse. In 1900 I went to work for Miller and Lux. Ed Turner was cattle superintendent and Rafael Cuen was cattle boss." Lou Ogden was superintendent for the southern division of Miller and Lux Ranches.

"In that year there were five chuck wagons at the Swan Well and seventy "bukeras" were fed from them. We had been gathering cattle for two months and we had twenty thousand head of cattle gathered.

"I worked on Poso Ranch when Jim Tunnell was boss there. Charlie Valenzuela was foreman. Oh, he was a fine 'bukera.' I never took down my reata when the Valenzuelas or the Felizes lassoed. It was no use. They never missed.

"I lived in Glennville for twenty years and never thought of locking the door. A man could ride from one end of the mountains to the other and never find a a door locked. But everybody locks up now, though that keeps only your friends out. People who steal will break down your door anyhow.

" 'Bukera' bosses quite often could neither read nor write; but they could count cattle as fast as they could be driven through a fifteen foot gate. They could also do sums in addition faster than a literate person could do them on paper. Rafael Cuen would fill his left hand with matches, take his position at a gate and count cattle as they galloped through. For every hundred he counted he would transfer a match from his left to his right hand. Sometimes he counted thousands, but he seldom if ever made a mistake no matter how many head or how fast they passed in front of him.

"The boys would often josh Cuen on how he got the job of cattle boss. Their version—entirely apocryphal, of course—was that there had been five herds of cattle gathered on the West Side. They had been gathered by five crews, each of which had a cattle boss in charge. Cuen had been one of the bosses. All the men and cattle were waiting for Henry Miller.

"One night when the other bosses were asleep Cuen took his vaqueros and parted all the poor steers out of his herd and put them in the other bosses' herds. He then parted out all the best steers in the other bosses' herds and put them in his herd. When Miller arrived Rafael had all the fat steers and the other bosses had poor ones. So Miller gave Cuen the job as cattle boss at Buttonwillow. Of course the story wasn't true and the boys told it just to needle old 'Jake' as he was called.

"But it only gave him the opportunity to brag about how Henry Miller had given him the job of boss when he was only twenty years old. It was true, he would say, that he had had the best steers; but he had gathered them all with his own crew.

"Those old men could recollect incidents which had occurred in their boyhood. Their accounts seemed to be pages torn from a diary written a half century before. Perhaps the reason their memories were so good was that their minds had never been crammed with book learning which was of no use to a vaquero; and as a result they had developed their own mental capacities."

THE LAZY MULE

It was the most beautiful mule that had ever been bred on that ranch. All through its colthood the mayordomo had watched over it. He intended it for his own use. When the mule was ready to go to the breaker, the mayordomo took her to the man himself and cautioned him about using care in handling her. He would even take the breaker a present of meat once in a while so that he would take special pains with her.

At long last the mule was finished and the breaker turned her over to the mayordomo. But that individual's disappointment was great when he found that the mule was lazy. He could hardly get her to steer out of her tracks. If he applied whip or spur the mule would kick up her hind legs and switch her tail, but she would never get out of a walk. So, in disgust he turned her over to the *arriero* who packed her with heavy loads, but she wasn't even good as a pack animal. When she had developed a big saddle sore over her kidneys the *arriero* was glad to turn her back to the mayordomo, who in turn looked for someone else on whom to foist the worthless animal. The only person among the vaqueros who would accept the mule was a big good-natured kid who could be easily imposed upon.

He accepted her without protest, but when he went to saddle her he found the big saddle sore. So he set about doctoring it. He got some tallow and cut it into small pieces, then he made a fire and fried it. When the grease was sufficiently cooled, as he thought, he poured it onto the sore on the mule's back, but the grease was hotter than he had thought. It burned the mule, causing her to kick, buck and wring her tail very vigorously.

Whether it was the grease that cured the sore or whether it healed in spite of it, we do not know; suffice it to say that the sore healed and the boy started riding the mule. One day he rode her into town. As he was passing the section of the town's plaza where food was sold, the mule started bearing on the bit and prancing with every indication that she wanted to run away from the sight or sound of that plaza.

Now it so happened that a mule buyer was sitting in the plaza. He had been a witness to the mule's odd behavior. He decided to see if he could buy her.

After inquiring he learned the name of the ranch from which the mule had come. He went there and without wasting time broached the subject of the mule to the *mayordomo*.

"Señor," he said, "I saw a mule in the plaza and was told to come to you. I am prepared to pay you three hundred *reales* for her."

The mayordomo would gladly have let the mule go for thirty *reales*, but was afraid there would be repercussions. So he said, "That mule is not worth even sixty *reales*. In fact she is worthless. I won't sell her."

But the buyer insisted. He had visions of selling her for three thousand *reales*. In the end, to get rid of him, the mayordomo sold him the mule at his own price.

The next day the buyer was back with the mule. He approached the mayordomo and said, "There must be something wrong with my way of riding. I can't get this mule out of a walk, and I saw her prancing in the plaza with the boy, Jose."

The mayordomo called Jose and told him to ride the mule to the plaza again. The two men went there and waited. Sure enough, when the mule passed the place where food was cooked and sold, she started prancing and bearing on the bit. The buyer said, "It must be the bit. I"ll change it." and went home with the mule. But the next day he was back again for the second time.

"I can't understand," he said, "I changed bits, but still the mule won't go."

The exasperated mayordomo called Jose and sent him to the plaza again. The results were the same. As the mule started prancing past the booths, it suddenly dawned on the mayordomo why the mule pranced. He called Jose and asked,

"Jose, what did you use to cure this mule's sore back?"

"Hot grease," the boy answered.

The mule had learned to associate the sound of frying cracklings with hot grease poured onto her sore back, so that whenever she heard the sound of them frying she would try to put as much distance as she could between her and that place of hot grease, as fast as she could.

PETE RIVERA

The first time I ever saw Pete Rivera was at a rodeo at Switzer's Grove, a place which has been out of existence for many years, and the reason I remember the event at all is that Pete rode a bucking horse. Bucking horses have become commonplace in the last fifty years, but that one stayed in my memory because Pete did something which is seldom done in riding a bucking horse. The horse threw him clear out of the saddle, but Pete managed to get back in again and ride the horse until the pick-up men pulled him off.

Pete is retired now and sits at home, perhaps dreaming of the days when he was an active vaquero on the great ranches. I went to pay him a visit, and our talk, as it never fails to do, turned to good horses, good reinsmen, and good breakers, their methods and ther ways with horses.

"When he rides the range," Pete said, "it is most important that a man know the country, because if a man doesn't, he will get lost, and the other vaqueros will laugh at him. Next in importance are good horses. If a man does not have good horses, he must train them as best he can. Each man has his own peculiar method of working and training a horse, and, more often than not, it is a good method for the man who uses it.

"Do you remember old Max Enderley who lived over on the desert next to the Tejon near Neenach? He and his brother bred horses on their ranch and broke them all themselves. The brothers must have come from some country where there were vaqueros, because they knew how to handle horses. They could ride anything that wore hair, but their horses for some reason or other, seldom bucked with them.

"They had an unusual knack with horses. They used a heavy, old, rusty ring bit—which they may have brought from Europe—on a colt from the first time they rode him, and pulled the bit just as one pulls a *jaquima*. If the colt bucked they would throw the reins at him and ride their balance, but as I have said, they were never bucked off, nor did they ever hurt the colt's mouth. When the colt had learned to rein, they would substitute a lighter, silver-mounted ring bit for the heavy one and go on riding the colt, but in spite of their unorthodox way of bitting, they turned out horses with good mouths.

"Whenever the brothers moved a band of mares they would never let the vaqueros help them. One of the brothers would start out and the mares would follow him.

"Max would move a band of mares from his place in Antelope Valley across the mountains to the Hill Ranch without anyone's help. The Indian vaqueros marveled at his ability to do this and believed that he used witchcraft to handle horses. But I could never account for his success in using the ring bits. He must have had a very light and delicate hand. I have never known anyone else who worked a horse that way.

"However, there were Indian vaqueros on the ranch who would start a colt in the *jaquima*, then when he was ready to go into the bit they would hang a heavy U.S. Army bit on him.

They, too, turned out some of the best-mouthed horses on the Tejon. Everyone knows that of all bits found on the ranches, the one with the most leverage is the Army bit. But Indians, as we all know, are patient, a virtue they acquired in the chase, when their living depended on stalking game.

"Indians, by the way, were much less severe with their horses than the whites. The whites used steel bits of different shapes, all more or less severe. They often cut a horse's tongue in two. The Indians wrapped or tied a rawhide thong around the horse's lower jaw, and while this may appear cruel, it is actually very mild. After a few minutes in a horse's mouth, the moisture would soften the rawhide and it would not hurt the animal. It is a very good system and why the vaquero did not adopt it more extensively is a mystery. Surely it is more effective than a *jaquima* and far less severe.

"The *bosal* (noseband) has its purpose, as do all the different pieces of the vaquero's equipment. They are vital to the handling of a horse, and the *bosal* is of major importance. Its purpose is to prevent the horse from opening its mouth too wide and dislocating its jaw when the animal is pulled. This happens when the bit has insufficient leverage and the rider has to pull with might and main to stop the horse.

"As we have said, different methods worked best with different men, and over a period of time each rider found the method best suited to him to work and turn out a horse most effectively. Some riders used a curb chain from the first time they bitted up a horse, and turned out some of the best-mouthed horses. Others used a curb strap exclusively, and also turned out good horses.

"However, it is my opinion that if a rider used a chain and a horse were to become "cold-jawed" (not respond to the pull on the bit) there would be no remedy. On the other hand, if a curb strap were used, then the horse could be softened up with a curb chain or a ring bit. Bits that were heavily coppered with rollers and copper striped mouthpieces tended to bring feeling back to a horse's mouth again.

"On one of the ranches there hung in the saddle room an old rusty ring bit. It did not seem to belong to anyone in particular, for everyone that needed it, used it. It was used mainly in the fall when the rodeos were over and the vaqueros were turning out their older horses to rest through the winter.

"Some vaqueros, in the experience of years and hard knocks, learned that a horse at the end of the roundup season will be very tired, and will have formed the habit of bearing on the bit for one reason or another, because he is tired and needs to brace himself, or needs the support of his rider, or his mouth has become numb and hard after going through so many days of mauling. Old vaqueros found that if a horse were turned out in the fall before he was softened up he would be hard when caught up in the spring. Consequently the vaquero would ride the horse with the ring bit until he had quit bearing on it. Then he would turn him out. The horse never failed to be normal again in the spring.

"A horse bucks for any reason, or for no apparent reason at all, and a horse can buck at any time, at just about anything; a puff of wind rustling the grass underfoot; a rabbit scurrying out of the brush, the shadow of a bird flying overhead. A horse often bucks because some vaquero, bent on mischief, will stick his toe into its flanks, or because of any of the ornery things one man is wont to do to get another rider bucked off.

"When a horse bucks on a ranch, it is not for the eight seconds that thrill spectators at Pendleton or Salinas. There are no pickup men ready to pull the rider off the bucker the instant the eight second whistle blows, and on the ranch there are no eight second whistles.

"The other vaqueros just sit their horses and watch the performance with a critical eye and await results. True sportsmen, they never interfere. They believe in both the man and the horse having an equal chance and a fair field. They like to see a horse buck long and hard; but by the same token, they like to see the man ride the horse. It thrills them no matter how often they have seen it or have been through the experience themselves. Besides, that is the only way to find out if a buckaroo is a good rider or if the horse is a good bucker. While the vaqueros may seem, in this respect, callous, still, a man who cannot ride has no business wearing boots and chaps. Their respect for a man who can ride is equal only to the respect and admiration for a horse that puts his heart into his work. Riding a long-bucking, crooked-bucking, hard-bucking horse is the best way for a man to gain the respect of the vaqueros with whom he works, and the best way to prove his riding ability."

Made in the USA
Lexington, KY
30 November 2018